Her History As She Wrote It

Compiled by Kerri

Copyright ©2018 MSL.KERRI
Sullivan Press/MSLKerri

24-G West Main St. Suite 364
Clinton, CT 06413

Email: MSL.KERRI@Gmail.com

*And she blew out the Candles
in memory of so many.*

Merissa Sherrill Lynn
Her History As She Wrote It

Index

Forward – by Kerri

History As She Wrote It:

Other published writings:

Obituary - December 2017

Acknowledgements

FORWARD

This collection of emails from Merissa Sherrill Lynn was sent to a small number of individuals to review, comment and advise her as she tried to put her history together. She posted via email more than 60 e-mails describing her life and some of the pressures around her. They include her vision and persons who influenced her life directions.

This book presents them without comment, changes, or alteration from the day she pressed the send key and sent them. The original recipients of her emails were people she trusted to give her honest and non-political feedback due to their urging   Merissa to tell her story.

As we know from the sheer volume of Merissa's writings in Rosebud, Tapestry, and many articles published worldwide it would be impossible to add all of this to the book. Instead, the author and several of the recipients of these emails wanted to keep this work to a readable and understandable collection of her writings so others might see, hear, and understand what went on in her career as a major leader of a movement to make a better world for all.

Merissa knew from her own experience the difficulties it is to come out, transition and dealing with the traumas of gender dysphoria, cross dressing and the manifestations of gender challenge. She wanted very much to help make everyone comfortable in their own skin irrespective of gender. This book can be read as individual stories or as a full story of her life remembered in her own words.

If you knew Merissa you know how hard she worked to build unity in a community many strong leaders. Her work gave those searching for a path something to follow. By these writings she also gives leaders of today's gender community things to remember and consider as they make their way through the pathways of leadership.

There are three special additions to her history and these are entered separately. Lady Slippers, Tribute to Ellen, and Candles have been added due to the personal nature of her writings.

In addition, the last pages include the obituary filed with newspapers after her passing in December of 2017, and an account of the spreading of her ashes on Mt. Washington with a Native American prayer in September 2018.

This author and helping friends hope you take away some of the magic we saw and loved in Merissa Sherrill Lynn.

Note: Lady Slippers, Tribute to Ellen, and Candles appeared in TV/TS Tapestry at various times.

Merissa's History parts 1 – 40

History Part 1

I was a child of the late '40's, the '50's, and a student of the '60's. It was a far more ignorant, bigoted, repressive and intoler- ant time than today.   To be raised in such a dogmatic and narrow- minded time was hard for a transsexual child, but my life was no more or less difficult than anybody else's.

Photo by   Mariette Pathy Allen

The thing I liked most about that time was there was more space to roam around in, clean- er air and more fish in the ocean. I didn't really know about prejudice at that time.   I didn't meet my first Catholic until I was in high school, my first person of a different race until I was a sophomore or my first Jew until I was a senior.   I was a basic, white Anglo Saxon Protestant Downeast Yankee.   I thought everybody was.   The only thing I knew about changing sex was from Mad Magazine when they made fun of Christine Jorgenson.   That magazine, as stupid and prejudi- cial as it was, did let me know that all things were possible.   I could hope, even if I was more ignorant than my beagle, or as they said in my neighborhood, dumber than a mackerel.

I don't really want to talk about my childhood.   There are dozens transsexual autobiographies out there, and they all sound like me.   For me to talk about me just seems redun- dant.   All my life I've had an intense desire to be female.   I didn't know why, and it was not important that I knew why. It was not important that anyone else knew why either. All that was important was that it was. My family knew it, and I knew it. They rejected me, I rejected them, and that was the end of that. With a few exceptions, that's the way it remains today, and that's the way it will remain. Today my family consists of the few members of my blood family that I love dearly, and a few members of the transgender community that I also love dearly.

As a child my heroes were Babe Didrikson, Calamity Jane, the Unsinkable Molly Brown and Sylvia Davis, a girl who lived in our trailer park. My family owned a trailer park. The thought of trailer parks and trailer park problems still gives me chills. Sylvia was my hero because she was beautiful and loving, could do anything, rough house with the best of us, be any way she wanted, and in the end still be the belle of the party. It tore me apart I was so jealous. I wanted to be her, right to the marrow of my soul I wanted to be her. Unfortunately, in my family having women as my heroes was not an acceptable thing, so, like so many of my brothers and sisters in the transgender community, I hid it

My favorite movies were Bambi and Peter Pan. My saddest movie scenes were when Bambi's mother was shot, and when Dumbo's mother was put in chains for trying to protect her baby. I was a natural born tree and animal lover, most at home in the woods, and was not a beat-em-up or shoot-em-down person. It wasn't in me to hurt or kill anything. It was in my father and brothers. To hide this discrepancy I was aloof, reasonably strong and a fair athlete, which was good enough to hide the 'female within' thing. For better or worse, I could play the 'masculinity' game to keep myself out of trouble. The problem with playing this phony game in order to stay safe and acceptable, was that it was toxic to my soul, and I didn't know if I would ever find a way to stop playing the game. In April, 1973, I found a way.

April, 1973. I walked into the Pemigewasset Wilderness in New Hampshire. It was a primordial woods, dark and damp, hidden by mountains. I was cold, tired and hungry. It was a mindless attempt at suicide. When I had gone as far as I could go, I had an epiphany. When I emerged from the wilderness I had an understanding my existence was natural, my life had value, and I had a purpose, to use the reality of my life to help others like myself, and in time to help the people whose lives we touch.

I spent the rest of 1973 trying to learn as much as I could about the cross-dressing/transsexual phenomena. Unfortunately, most of what I could find had to do with erotica which didn't teach me anything useful, and was of no value. That year I met Sherry, who became my friend, my support and my love. She was the first person other than myself to tell me who and what I was, was all right.

In my searches for information I came across Dr. Harry Benjamin's book 'the Transsexual Phenomena', and Virginia Prince's book 'Understanding Cross-dressing'. These books gave me enough valid information to begin lecturing on the college classroom level. In 1974, while conducting a lecture at the University of New Hampshire, I was outed by the ultra-right wing newspaper 'the Manchester Union Leader'. The article was not prejudicial or mean, but it did put me in danger both domestically and professionally, and forced me to confront my demons publicly. The incident proved to be a positive experience both at home and at work. As a professional ski instructor, the 1974/1975 season became my most successful in an eleven year career.

May, 1975. After watching a television program featuring Deborah Feinbloom, author and director of the Gender Identity Service, and Ariadne Kane, director of the Outreach Institute, I found and joined a Boston social and support group, called Cherrystone. Cherrystone was a place I could be comfortable and simply be myself. It was also a place I could begin to help others. The difficulty was Cherrystone consisted mostly of closeted cross-dressers who wanted a private and secure location where they could be with friends, cross-dress and enjoy themselves. It was a difficult atmosphere in which to accomplish anything. Fortunately I met Ariadne Kane, who not only was director of the Outreach Institute, was also planning a social and educational event Fantasia Fair, which was to be held in Provincetown in the fall. I volunteered to help in any way I could.

October, 1975. I attended and assisted in my first transgender event. Next to my epiphany in the Pemigewasset Wilderness, Which put an end to my desire for oblivion and gave my life meaning, my first Fantasia Fair was my most important incident. It brought me out of my closet, helped me overcome my fear of public exposure, put me to work, and taught me what I needed to know if I was ever to do any good. It also introduced my to wonderful people, both members of our community and civilians, people who would be influential in my future efforts.

The 1975/1976 ski season continued on from the previous year, and was again successful. During the season I made contact with a number of the staff from TV's Channel Four. Among these was Pat Mitchell who hosted her own talk show, the same talk show that hosted Deborah Feinbloom and Ariadne Kane. I was invited to be her guest, and thus began a long string of television appearances.

1976 was a good year, the best I ever had up to that time. Sherry and I had a grand romp all year. My sister Sylvia was doing a fine job managing my family's trailer park, and as a seamstress was doing considerable outreach within the transgender community. I continued doing college class-room lectures, a few television appearances and radio pro-grams, cross-dressed with confidence and without fear. That was a very long way from the previous year.

Cherrystone moved from its tiny little hovel to a larger more private apartment. The problem was no one wanted to sign the lease. This allowed a person with more fetishistic lean-ings to live there, and use the apartment for her own inter-ests. This attracted some and alienated others, creating two separate groups, providing me the opportunity to create. I began working on long-term objectives and a strategy to achieve those objectives.

The objective was to focus on outreach, education and sup-port, and to build a community. The primary values would be: pride, dignity, respect (for others and for self), family (caring for and about each other), community, and working together for the benefit of all.

Gloria Wright, a friend from Chicago, coined the term Sym-biotic Synergism, meaning different people brought together by circumstance into a common environment, working to-gether for the benefit of all. That catchy little termed defined community as well as any I had ever heard.

My problem was to find a strategy that would overcome what I considered society's value system, which was arrogance (masculine or social superiority complex, and a caste system based on special interest), sex (sex sells, but that is all), vanity (ego gratification), greed (profit as the bottom line rather than service), and meanness (the end justifies the means no matter how cruel). To find a strategy I needed dreamers, which were hard to find. Diane was perfect for that. She was not only a dreamer, but she had a business sense I was sorely lacking.

Diane was a CPA, so our early conversations went something like:

Me: We need to do some outreach to find good people willing to work with us.   *Diane*: $$$$$$$$$$$$$$

Me: We might start thinking about a house to rent where the folks can come and dress, leave their wardrobes, live if necessary, socialize, where we can hold classes, parties, etc.
Diane: $$$$$$$$$$$$$$$$$$$$$$$

Me: We might think about buying our own house, and perhaps using that as capital for other ventures, such as other houses, our own guest house or houses, our own lounge, etc.
Diane: $$$$$$$$$$$$$$$$$$$$$$$$$$$$

Me: We could start our own trust fund to support educational projects, hot lines, offices, and staff. We could create our own business enterprise, give our people places to live, jobs, provide an income for whatever projects we wish to do, retreats, educational conventions, research Libraries, magazines, coffee table books, our own publishing house, a community bank, etc.   Well, it's something to think about.

Our planning was just talk, but it sure fired the imagination. It was hard to stay focused when everything was possible, and I wanted it all.   The trick was to figure out how to make it happen. First things, first. We needed to build a local cadre of like-minded supporters.

At the end of 1976, I received some very sad news. Sherry had cancer. She had to return to her family, for they had the means to support her. I was alone.

History part 4

When Sherry left I fell into a depression darker than any I had known. The 1976/1977 ski season was pretty much the same, with more requested private lessons than assigned classes. Every Wednesday I made the three hour commute from Waterville Valley to Boston. Sometimes I went straight from work to Cherrystone still wearing my ski boots, and instructor's uniform. Being in urban Boston surrounded by cross-dressers, while wearing ski boots, parka, and sweater felt a little odd.

1977 was pretty much like 1976. The year's project was on behalf of Ariadne Kane's Outreach Institute. I spent the entire summer visiting every commercial establishment that might have any interest to our community. The intention was to create a TV shopper's guide to Boston. The most hostile reactions were indifference. I had a few special requests, such as wear clean socks before trying on shoes, and a few enthusiastic receptions, especially from a couturier on Newbury Street, Boston's most fashionable shopping area, and Gladys Talbot, an elderly corset maker on Massachusetts Avenue. Gladys became a close friend for many years. As did Eleanor Cohen, manager of Wig Wam in Downtown Crossing, the primary shopping district in Boston. In time Eleanor became a partner of Image Consultants, which openly welcomed cross-dressers, and eventually owned a private wig fitting service.

The lesson I learned from this exercise was if our people exercised good manners and common sense, we were welcome most anywhere. Commercial establishments can be very welcoming when it comes to making money.

After my exercise with the shopping guide, it was back to normal, trying to build support for future projects, back to work for Fantasia Fair, then back to the mountains. That winter I was transferred from Waterville's main mountain, to Mount Snow, a smaller mountain in the valley. I was the only instructor, so I had private lessons from opening to closing, and since Mount Snow was used for night skiing, and for our school's torchlight parades, I would work nights as well. I was getting bloody sick of skiing.

In May 1978 I sent out my first letter of intent. It detailed my battle plan for the development of a new social organization to be located in my home. That letter would become a monthly newsletter, and would eventually evolve into the 'TV-TS Tapestry. I began holding social gatherings for the folks I hoped would be the cadre for future projects. From that group came Pat and Marcie, who remain among my dearest friends to this day.

In November 1978 we had a meeting at my house to create a constitution for our group. We declared ourselves a non-profit group. Diane wanted to make sure we would eventually become eligible for 501 (C) 3 status, tax exempt status, which would make membership fees and contributions tax deductible. That would be a major step towards legitimacy.

We had no idea what to call ourselves. We had silly suggestions, such as 'the Spank N Hanky club, and Pat suggested 'SMUT', sexy men in undies and tights. Other suggestions included 'New England TV Coalition', 'Chantilly', 'the Champagne Club', 'Tiffany', and 'Carousel'. Tiffany and Carousel were both names of championship tea roses. We settled on the name 'Genesis'. Unfortunately, some business somewhere was already called Genesis, so we settled 'the Tiffany Club'.

I had recently received word that Sherry succumbed to her disease. I could not think of her without crying. On my wall hung a photo Sherry had given to me. It was a picture of a man's hand interlocked with a woman's hand, holding a single red rose. To me it was beautiful, symbolic of the masculine and the feminine united in nature, similar to the oriental interlocking teardrops of Yin and Yang, a perfect logo for the Tiffany Club, and for whatever other projects would come along. It also was very personal to me, and would always remind me of Sherry, and would always leave a lump in my throat.

History part 5

At the 1978 Fantasia Fair, Ariadne put me in charge of the consignment shop. There was no one I could think of less qualified to run a consignment shop. I was strictly a dungaree and sweatshirt kind of gal, and had no clue, but that's what I was asked to do, so I did the best I could. I received complaints aplenty for overpricing, underpricing, and simply not knowing what I was doing. For some reason I completely failed to understand, I was voted 'Most Helpful'. I was not going to be available on the evening I was to be acknowledged, so my sister Sylvia, who at the time was in a relationship with a cross-dresser, borrowed an evening dress from her boyfriend, and accepted the award on my behalf.

After the Fair and the formation of the Tiffany Club, I returned to the mountains for the last time. I was not a great skier, but I was a good teacher, so I got all the people who needed a good teacher. That meant beginners. After eleven seasons of beginners, averaging eight to ten hours a day on a pair of skis, literally spending more time on the beginner's

J-bar than the lift attendants, for 135 consecutive days from November to April each year, and with the transgender projects taking shape, it was definitely time to retire from skiing. When I returned from the hills I began getting hints of future problems. I started getting buffeted by special interests. Especially vigorous were those who wanted Tiffany to become a Tri Sigma (now Tri Ess) chapter, and cater exclusively to heterosexual cross-dressers. That meant since I was transsexually inclined, I would have been banned from my own organization. Since I admitted to being transsexually inclined but refused to label myself transsexual, I had already been banned from the XX Club, a transsexual support group in Hartford. Since I refused to label myself as anything, most people just assumed I was a cross-dresser. Wrong! Some wanted Tiffany to just be a party club. The hedonistic retreat for libertines. Some just wanted to make money. Special interests were rearing their ugly heads.

I also began being challenged from within the club for my lack of business expertise. I offered to turn over the office and financial matters to anyone with more "business expertise", but there were no takers. It seemed they just wanted to complain, and not to actually do anything about it. I was also criticized from around the nation for my "My way or the highway" attitude. They were right. It was my way or the highway. I would not focus on any particular special interest group, and did not want to with or for anyone who did not share a common vision and was not willing to work together for the benefit of all. I wanted to build a community, to help as many people as possible. To accomplish that I needed to build a cadre of like minded people working together for a common objective. I needed to build a community of people working together for a common objective. By having a common vision, and a common focus, and common effort, we could help everyone.

Then I was challenged, by people who did not trust my motives. They claimed I wanted to be empress of the whole shooting match, I wanted power, I wanted the money, etc. I tried to explain I had lived my life without purpose. The acknowledgement and acceptance of my transsexuality gave my life purpose, and a desire to use my spirit to help other people. I had no interest in being the boss. I had no interest in money. I just wanted to do as much good as I could. It seemed there was a gathering cloud of obstacles.

At the 1979 Fair, in the Madeira Room of the Pilgrim House, I sang a song I had written for Sherry. It was not a very good song, and I had a difficult time singing it, but I needed to sing it. When it was finished I received a standing ovation, which shocked me.

Also in 1979 my mother passed. When she died the trailer park was sold, and I needed to decide what to do with my inheritance. The choice was to either use it to take care of my needs, or use it to help people for as long as I could. I chose to use it. I could use it to keep myself alive until whenever. The next thing I could use it for was since my home was gone, Tiffany needed a new home. Fortunately, Diane had been looking, and found a house in Weston Massachusetts to rent. I could subsidize the house until it was self-supporting. The next thing I could use it for was to develop the Tapestry into a magazine. I had editing experience, but no publishing experience, which presented challenges.

History part 6

Our house in Weston was perfect for our needs at the time. Large enough for parties and meetings, private enough for people with security issues, a large basement for those with storage issues, classy enough for those with dignity issues, reasonable office space to work, produce the Tapestry, for hotlines, etc., and near to private locations to meet and interview new people, and we had a good relationship with the authorities. Many times I would receive phone calls from the police saying, "Merissa, we have one of yours down here. Come and get her." Usually a drunk driver, or occasionally somebody doing something stupid like wearing a nightie into the local market.

For me personally, I loved the location because we were surrounded by history. We were on the original Boston Post Road, down the road a piece from Longfellow's Wayside Inn. We were next door to the Golden Ball Tavern where General Knox rested after hauling the cannon from Fort Ticonderoga on his way to Dorchester Heights to drive the British out of Boston. The Tavern was next to a beautifully manicured Revolutionary War graveyard filled with fascinating and intricately carved slate gravestones complete with Betsy Ross flags. Across the street was the row of the original sycamore trees beneath which Knox's troops rested. History was everywhere, 18th century stone churches and stone walls, and 19th century town halls and courtyards. The picturesque town square was later used as the town square in the 1994 movie 'Little Women'.

Unfortunately when we moved in we were midst the worst gypsy moth infestation of the century. Everything, the house, the trees, even the mailbox was covered with egg sacks. Also, the owner wanted to sell the house. Being in Weston, the most expensive town in Massachusetts, the price was way beyond our means, which meant we had to start planning our next move. That necessity caused me to create NACD Inc., an investment corporation. NACD was fully incorporated, with stocks and everything. The initials, NACD didn't stand for anything, whatever the people writing checks wanted to call it. I called it Naked Inc.

I thought NACD was potentially my best idea. I had little trouble finding investors, although I was personally the primary investor. With money we could do anything, starting with a small retreat for our people. From there we could own our own guest houses, housing for people in transition or simply in need of a place to live, recreational facilities, offices, publisher's clearing house, gender clinics, a community bank, just about anything we could have thought of. We could have provided jobs to our people who needed them.

There were plenty of people willing to offer advice, but they left it to me, the person without business expertise, to run it. The results were predictable. I was already managing the Tiffany Club, editing and publishing the Tapestry, coordinating and directing the parties, the outings and social functions, and doing outreach, lectures, the hotline service, and so on. I had no mind or will to run a business enterprise of that magnitude. It was overwhelming. We had qualified people, but I couldn't get them involved, beyond buying a few shares of stock.

We did manage to purchase the Wayland House, but that's where it ended. To my dying day I will consider NACD to have been of the greatest potential service to our community, and the decline of NACD to be my greatest failure.

History part 7

Although we were only in our Weston home for a very short time, from November 1979 to July 1981, we managed to achieve a great deal. Our membership exploded. We had members from Japan, Indonesia, Australia, South Africa, Egypt, Saudi Arabia, Estonia, and all over North and South America. We created NACD and had staggering dreams of what we could do for our people. The Tapestry grew from a club newsletter to a crude magazine, with mailings all over the world, to members, mental health professionals, and business professionals.

Tiffany had attracted a number of members who were truck drivers. At one time we would have a driveway full of pickup trucks, an 18-wheel car carrier, an 18-wheel Rich's Department Store truck, and a Boston Globe delivery truck. It was an odd sight to see on a quiet street in Weston. We resembled an Interstate 81 truck stop. No one complained, so it wasn't a problem, however the Weston police did drive by shaking their heads.

We were able to assist and support Outreach Institute's projects, Fantasia Fair, and Boutique Fantastique. During Fantasia Fair, we had a hurricane the night of the awards banquet. Many of the participants were trapped in their respective buildings, the restaurant on the roof of the Crown & Anchor blew off, crushing cars and wrapping itself around a telephone pole. Dinner that night was prepared with propane torches, and it was delicious. We ate by candlelight, and we all looked a shambles. The best story was a Tiffany Club couple, Donna and Michelle, were in attendance. Donna was pregnant. Her water broke while she was dancing at the Pied Piper. They rushed her to the nearest hospital that had power, which was in Hyannis, nearly a two hour drive from Provincetown. Donna delivered a beautiful baby girl, named Michelle.

I always wanted to be a fly on the wall when Donna explained to her daughter the circumstances of her birth. "Well, Honey, your father and I were at a convention for transvestites. We were dancing in a lesbian bar, when we were hit by a hurricane. The power went out, and you decided to get born. Since the power was out we had to travel two hours to a hospital that had power. You were born, and we named you Michelle, after your father."

The Hartford TVIC facilities burned down, and we were able to provide tangible support for its members. As with Outreach, it was the first time two different transgender organizations worked together for the benefit of their members.

We had dreams for the Tapestry as well, for it to be a primary source of outreach and up-to-date information, to be a communication medium and unifying device for the entire community, to keep improving its quality until it became a collectable and worthy of being placed on the coffee table. It would be a source of pride, integrity and dignity for our people. It was to be a dignified way to present our community to the world.

We became involved in the Gay community's hotline training program, and the speaker's bureau, and developed our own speaker's bureau. We became very active in getting our story out to the public and media.

I created Tiffany's awards, and Awards Banquet, which evolved into Tiffany's First Event, a program which continues to this day. I also created Tiffany's Annual Spring Fling in Provincetown. It was an event created just for the fun of it, and eventually grew to an enormous size for a transgender event.

We continued with bi-weekly meetings, and monthly parties. In just a short year and a half, Tiffany had become a very busy organization, and I had become exhausted. Then we moved, and became busier than ever.

History part 8

We purchased a house in Wayland Massachusetts. The house suited our needs, roomy and secluded with lots of privacy and parking, and the location was beautiful, overlooking the Sudbury River which meant gorgeous sunsets and a wonderful river for canoeing. The house abutted the Great Meadows National Wildlife Refuge, and was surrounded by scenic nature trails. One of these trails was an AMC trail that circumnavigated Greater Boston, from the South Shore, around the Rte 128 perimeter to the North Shore. What I did not realize was as beautifully located as the house was, it was also located on a flood plain. Another thing they did not tell me was during times of floods they dammed the river to keep larger towns downstream from getting flooded. In time we paid the price for that ignorance.

When it came time to move from Weston to Wayland, we had a goodly number of volunteers, with a goodly number of trucks, but we didn't use the car carrier. Once we settled into our new home, a housewarming party was called for. We had a lot of housewarming gifts, mostly booze. I didn't drink, but did manage to slip away with a bottle of Amaretto and a bottle of Southern Comfort. It lasted me for years. After the party I ran headlong into the same problem I did at Cherrystone.

I gathered the NACD stockholders to discuss the next step. What next step? They seemed to have forgotten that the Wayland House was just supposed to be the first step. They were happy with the status quo. When I talked with the Tiffany Club board of directors, it was the same thing. After years of work, and spending money to build a community, All I had managed to achieve was to buy a lot of equipment, create a small social local club, create a newsletter for that club, run a few parties and get-aways, and acquire a retreat for that club. I wasn't interested in catering to one small group of local people. I was interested in gathering a cadre of like-minded people with vision, with a desire to help more people than just themselves, build a community, and provide that community with the tools that would enable that community to unify, and to work together for the benefit of all, including society as a whole. I kept running into roadblocks, and couldn't make it happen. I couldn't even develop an effective hostess program where I wasn't the only one doing interviews, and newcomers wouldn't be isolated and ignored. It was very frustrating, and I faced my first case of severe burn-out. I really really wanted to say "The hell with it," and go my own way. The problem was I had no way to go, so the only alternative was to keep on keeping on.

My first effort was to appear on the Tom Cottle show. Tom was a psychologist with his own television program. Tom asked me a great question for which I had no answer. He asked, "If you don't like men, why did you work for what is essentially a men's club?" It was not a question I was prepared to answer, and I fumbled with weak answers such as the arrogance of assigning God a masculine gender, despicable masculine superiority complexes, macho behavior, etc. When I got home I thought about his question and wrote him a long letter. The conclusion of that letter was, "If you break down a man's macho armor and scratch his soul, you just might find a beautiful human being. Some of the most beautiful women in the world are men, and some of them belong to the Tiffany Club."

History part 9

An adjunct to the Tom Cottle show: the producer of the show was Debbie Lathrop, who had made arrangements for me to appear on several shows. My niece, who's name was also Debbie, had made arrangements for a visit. When my niece called from the airport for me to come and pick her up, I mistook her for Debbie Lathrop. The conversation that followed was truly bizarre. There was me wondering why Debbie Lathrop was calling me for a ride from the airport, and there was my poor niece sitting alone in the airport wondering what my appearances on television had to do with giving her a ride from the airport, and profoundly confused by my thanking her for her efforts. My niece was patient and finally got through to me who she was, which made me feel like an incomprehensible ass. On my way to the airport, a trip I had made dozens of times, I got turned around and ended up going over a rusty relic of a bridge and found myself in downtown Charlestown, miles from the airport. I managed to turn a 30 minute ride into a 3 hour ride, again making me feel like a complete ass. To top things off, when I got to the airport, I hadn't seen Debbie since she was a baby, didn't know what she looked like, and couldn't find her. That fixed it, I was a complete ass. Debbie found me, but she must have thought her uncle was truly peculiar.

After my disappointment with the NACD investors and Tiffany board of directors, and reflections after my letter to Tom Cottle, I found my dreams were no longer a possibility, and needed to reassess my long term objectives and strategy to achieve those objectives.

The first thing I did was forget about trying to use Tiffany to build a cadre of like-minded people working together to build a community. The best I could hope for was a cadre of people willing to throw a party. The next thing I did was dissolve NACD, buy the house myself, which used up the last of my personal resources, and pay off the investors. After that I was on my own. I rented rooms to transgendered people who needed a supportive place to live, and rented the use of the facility to the Tiffany Club for storage, functions, etc. I no longer trusted anyone to be farsighted enough to work together for the future.

The 1981 Fantasia Fair, by which time I had become its coordinator, was to be my last Fair. The Fair had become elitist and a "candy machine" to finance the Outreach Institute, which was in turn focused on working with mental health professionals. It was a niche that needed to be filled but it was not my niche. I would continue to support the Fair, for it certainly served a purpose, but I would switch my attention to running a good social club, improving the Tapestry, and building on Tiffany's other projects, such as educational programs, social events, outreach, the hotline, the hostess program, the speaker's bureau, First Event and the Spring Fling.

1982 proved to be one of our most memorable years, but it started off with a disaster. We were preparing for our awards banquet, which by that time had grown into a week-end long program. At that time I was a bit apelike, covered with hair. To remove the hair, I used Zip Wax, blocks of it. I was melting a pot of it in my room when for some reason I was distracted. I promptly forgot it until everything I touched became sticky and a gooey fog floated down from my room. I dashed upstairs to find my five pound pot of was had been vaporized and everything, and I do mean every-thing, my bed, wardrobe, books, papers, floor, walls, furni-ture, dishes, food, everything, upstairs and down, was cov-ered in a sticky waxy veneer. It not only covered everything I owned, but everything everyone else owned, and was im-possible to remove. I still have books that are covered with wax to this day.

1982 also provided me with one of my favorite quotes. We were preparing for our Saint Patrick's party, my dear friend Pat and I went to dinner. In celebration of the event I tried the Irish coffee. I about choked, and asked Pat, "Why does this stuff have to taste like creosote?" Without batting an eyelash she responded, "Because we can't trust the saints to preserve us." I thought my accident with the wax had done a pretty good job of that, but her comment still gives me a chuckle.

After the party, before our April clean-up party we were hit with another disaster. We had gathered all our rakes, wheel barrows, wood chippers and such, when we were hit by a

Nor'easter. The spring blizzard dumped 18 inches of rock-hard snow on us, which when it melted, flooded our basement. No real damage done, other than a few wet rugs.

History part 10

We moved our spring outing to June. It was warmer, and all the stores and restaurants were open. Unfortunately, it rained in biblical proportions the entire time. It was the first time I had been to a cross-dresser's event where the most popular item was an umbrella. That meant the party moved indoors, and chose my room to party in. It was a madhouse. The outing was wildly successful in spite of the weather. After the outing we returned home to find our beautiful backyard and pool were submerged in the Sudbury River. Our basement was also submerged. We lost our wardrobes which were in storage, and for me the real tragedy was we lost our library. We had collected every publication of every organization in our community. It made me heartsick to lose all that history. The flood gave the remnants of the outing a chance to keep the party going, which they did for a week, and it gave Dorothy a chance to show off her ability to put a drink on her head, sink to the floor, do ten pushups and rise up again without spilling a drop. The talent in our community was, at times, staggering.

When the water receded, our yard looked like Rye Beach at low tide after a hurricane. Every bit of flotsam and jetsam in the river chose our yard to settle. It was a frightening mess. Out came the rakes, wheelbarrows and wood chipper, and as a group we got it clean. We had to work as a group, which we did, and we were successful, which pleased me. It always pleased me to see members of our community working together for the common good. That meant I didn't have to do all the work myself.

The social event of the year involved Diane. I met Diane when I first emerged into the community, and she had been my working partner ever since. She wrote our constitution and secured our non-profit tax exempt status. She found our home in Weston. Tiffany would never have been a successful organization without her. On July 17, 1982, Diane and Char got married, and chose our backyard as the site. Fortunately we had a minister in our membership, and she was willing to perform the ceremony. We had a huge crowd for the event, including our neighbors. The wedding was just wonderful. Their wedding was neither a fantasy nor symbolic. To my knowledge, Diane and Char's wedding was the first real transgender wedding, where both the bride and the groom were cross-dressed, the minister was cross-dressed, and all the guests with the exception of the neighbors were cross-dressed. It was a historical event for Tiffany.

After my disappointment with the NACD investors and the Tiffany board of directors, I was very discouraged, and prone to depression, but I decided to give building a cadre of leaders one more try. I felt like a match trying to ignite a fire that would not burn. A match alone was not a fire. I put out a call for the development of an annual leader's conference to be held at Fantasia Fair. I called for people who were already in a leadership position within the transgender community, for people who were interested in becoming leaders, and active supporters. I rekindled my hope to build a cadre of leaders who would work together to build a community.

I established a place for our meetings, the Chicago House on Winslow Street in Provincetown, planned the itinerary and set the agenda, then wondered who would show up. I showed up (representing Tiffany). Others who were there included Betty Ann (Mid-Atlantic, GGA), Naomi (Tri-Ess,

Chicago), Maxine (Delta Chapter, Texas), Winnie (Albany TVIC), Janna (Shangri La, California), Joan (San Jose, GGA), Rachia (New England TS Support), Shivon and Shalon (XX Club, Hartford), Deborah (FACT, Ontario), Paula (Halcyon, Rhode Island), Sandy (Delta Chi, Virginia), Elaine (Crossroads, Michigan), Elaine (Nu, North Carolina), Carolyn (DREAM, Oregon), Helen (Beaumont, England), and several independent supporters.   To me it was a wonderfully diverse representation.

The agenda for the program was to get to know each other, brainstorm problem areas and areas that needed improvement, then isolate those topics that could most productively be discussed throughout the week. The seven topics that emerged were: 1) how to better handle inquiries, specially inquiries concerning other organizations, 2) screening people, 3) How do you deal with people looking for legitimate social contacts, 4) how do we deal with the P.O. Box Phenomena, 5) if an international organization were possible, what would be the nature of that organization, and how would it survive 'the changing of the guard'. The last two topics were, 6) how do we acquire additional facilities such as Tiffany's, and how to we finance and maintain them, and 7) the development of a directory to serve the community, and what would be the nature of such a directory, how would it be developed and maintained.

To me it all sounded like stuff I had been working on for the previous seven years.   It also sounded suspiciously like whatever they came up with, I was going to get stuck doing it, especially when it dealt with issues that could best be handled by the Tapestry, and with Tiffany. NACD was already dead with no hope of resurrection, and the Tiffany Board of Directors buried in their own issues. However, we came together as a community, and talked. It couldn't have been better.

The '82 Fantasia Fair not only provided me an opportunity to coordinate a leadership conference, it provided me with my most emotional and memorable experience in the transgender community. My dear friend Frances was paying the price for a lifetime of alcohol abuse. She was dying, and she knew it. The many friends she had made in Provincetown over the years also knew it. For the FanFair Follies, Frances and Dorothy had cooked up a routine. The night of the Follies, Frances was escorted up on stage by another dear friend, Pat.

The applause was loud and continuous. Frances stood by her piano, faced the audience, and said, "In the words of the late great Al Jolson, "you ain't heard nothin' yet." She sat and prepared to hammer out a tune when Dorothy, dressed as Mae West, came up on stage. Prior to their performance Dorothy had placed a large scroll on the wall. Dorothy unrolled the scroll, upon which were the lyrics to 'Rosie'. She turned to the audience and began directing the audience in a 'Mitch Miller type follow the bouncing ball' sing-along. With arms linked and bodies swaying and 300 people singing at the top of their lung power, the song quickly turned from singing for the fun of it, into a farewell tribute to Frances. Frances thought she and Dorothy were going to perform 'Rosie' for the audience. Instead, with Dorothy egging them on, the audience was performing 'Rosie' for Frances. She understood and turned to receive her tribute. Everyone, 300 people strong, were singing as if their hearts were going to break. I began crying like a little girl. Everyone did. The people of Provincetown were saying goodbye and thank you.

During my first visit to Cherrystone in 1975, Frances was one of the first people I met. She introduced herself as a 5'5" ugly old man and a 5'9" sporty old lady, reflecting her penchant for spiked heeled boots, and made me feel welcome.

Her music and her laughter lit up the room and made friends wherever she went. Frances was an extraordinary spirit, and an adored member of our community. On January 14, 1983 Frances died.

I believed the leadership conference left me with a mandate, to build the Tapestry into a unifying device for the community. That meant the Tapestry would become an international publication, transcending the Tiffany Club. That also meant making sure everyone who needed accurate and up-to-date information would get it, and coordinating the information from everyone who could give me that up-to-date information. It was a frightening responsibility, and a lot of work. Maintaining a directory of organizations and services, editing, publishing and distributing the Tapestry, managing the Tiffany Club and the house, coordinating the parties and outings, and maintaining the hotline and speaker's bureau, was seriously overwhelming. A personal failing made itself manifest. It was very difficult for me to ask for help. If I was supposed to be a leader, that was not a very beneficial trait to have.

If I couldn't ask for help the least I could do is thank those that did. Therefore I created the Awards Banquet, and the awards, and presented them at the banquet. The awards were created to develop a sense of family, community and pride. The awards were: 'the Secretary's Award' for the most outstanding overall contribution to Tiffany, 'the Most Helpful Award' for the person most ready and willing to help when help was needed, 'the Miss Tiffany Award' voted on by the membership on the basis of dignity and ladylike demeanor, 'the Friendship Award' for helping new people feel welcome and comfortable, 'Special Recognition Awards' for people who made outstanding contributions to the success of a Tiffany event, and 'Certificates of Appreciation' for everyone who needed to be thanked.

Since I created the awards and presented them, the chances of me ever receiving an award was pretty slim. However, a few members got together and presented me with a 'Whining, Bitching and Complaining' award. It was a category which I had not considered.

During my time in the community it was my pleasure (I'm not sure if pleasure is the right word) to meet some strange characters. Among the strangest most unchaste and profligate characters I knew was a person we came to know as Lambchops. He was everywhere, at every party especially in Provincetown. When he began to fade from the scene, one of our members, Malinda, who found Lambchops amusing, suggested we place Lambchops on the 'Protected Species' list, gave him the Latin name Lambchopus Libertinis P-townus', and formed the Lambchops International Preservation Society (LIPS). She described him as, "The Lambchopus is a rare and exotic species noted for its licentious behavior and impressive plumage. This creature must be saved. The loss of such a libido would be a true loss. Save the Lambchopus!" LIPS never took off, and Lambchops became extinct.

History part 12

At the 1982 FanFair Follies, I sang a song written by Elaine Willey of Michigan's Crossroads Chapter. The tune was written to Gilbert and Sullivan's 'I am the very model of a modern major general'. Its title was 'I am the very model of a modern paraculturalist', and contained lines like "I'm very well acquainted to with matters of androgyny, I plan to leave a brood of genderally unclear progeny." To quote Elaine, "the song was written to poke fun at the contemporary move towards categorical loquaciousness." To me the song was hysterical, but the situation was not. New terms and new meanings of old terms kept flowing into the community, to the point where nobody knew what the hell any body was saying. If we couldn't communicate with each other, we had no chance of communicating with the world.

For instance, the term 'transgender' was a word coined by Virginia Prince to replace the word transvestite. Virginia wanted a word she could apply to the members of her organization (FPE) that did not carry the sexual overtones of transvestite. She wanted 'transgender' to identify people who were comfortable expressing themselves in both masculine and feminine terms. The term evolved to identify people who cross-lived without identifying as transsexual, or considering sexual reassignment surgery (SRS). Eventually 'transgender' evolved into an umbrella term covering everyone and everything related to the cross-dressing/transsexual phenomena. The term had become so generic and meaningless that it became useful again. For instance, I originally called the Tapestry the TV/TS Tapestry. It is now called 'the Transgender Tapestry'. Our community was originally called the TV/TS community. It is now called 'the Transgender Community'. It still doesn't mean anything, but it's easy to understand.

I was at a planning meeting for the "Rainbow Coalition" parade in Washington DC. There was no debate as to whether or not to include gay, lesbian and bisexual people, but they had no idea what to call the rest of us. Cross-dressers, transvestites, transsexuals, drag queens, or what. Everyone wanted their own little group identified, but it would never fit on the flag, or some such thing. Then someone suggested 'transgender', but because it was still identified with Virginia Prince's homophobic philosophy, no one wanted to be called that. I was asked what I thought. I responded that no one liked transgender, which was the closest we were going to get on a consensus about anything, so we may as well use it. We used it. the Rainbow Coalition became known as GLBT (gay, lesbian, bisexual, transgender), which fit nicely on the flag.   I tried to fix the situation, or possibly add to the problem, and I compiled a directory of terms.   I focused on keeping it simple and common sense, and began with the basics, such as defining 'category',   the difference between 'biology' and 'psychology', the difference between 'sex' and 'gender',   'male/female'   and   'masculine/feminine', cross-dressing Transgender/ transsexual/ drag, and so on.   I tried to write it in such a way that it could be constantly edited and updated. That way our community would have an easy reference for new comers, lectures, and most importantly communication.   The directory met with some success, but nowhere near what I had hoped.

True story lifted from our 'Not So Domestic' department: Our laundry room was in the basement.   Kim (Colorado) was trying to do her laundry, with no success.   I overheard Patricia, one of our residents, talking to Kim.   "There may be many reasons why this washing machine doesn't work.   It could be broke, the belt could be loose, or you're trying to use it incorrectly.   However, I think the reason this washing machine doesn't work is because it's the dryer."

History part 13

The 1983 Spring Outing was pretty much the same as usual, only a lot more people.   There was the usual meet-and-greet mixers, lots of food, whale watching, shopping, exploring, and above all, partying.   However, this outing provided me with some of my fondest memories.   What pleased me most was how well our old-timers took care of the first-timers.   To my knowledge no one felt left out or ignored, and never had to go eat alone.   I was proud of my kids.

We also had some interesting guests.   Bebe Scarpi, VP of Lee's Mardi Gras Boutique in NYC, was in attendance.   She had never attended a function other than Lee's.   She was there to meet people, have fun, and scout for an event Lee was planning for the fall. Lee was such a great help to me when I first emerged from my closet, and had done so much for so many others, that I told Bebe that I would be more than happy to help her and Lee with their event in any way I could. Fred Barry of the Transvestian was there to get the whole report for his newspaper, and Mariette Allen, an old friend from my third Fantasia Fair, and a photographer from NYC was there to document the event.

In third place of my favorite memories was a group dinner. We gathered up everyone and took over a local restaurant which featured singing waiters. We were enjoying a fine dinner when the waiter began singing the Beatles song 'Yesterday'. When the waiter got to the line, "Suddenly, I'm not half the man I used to be..", a high pitched giggle emanated from the corner. It was from Priscilla, a very attractive transsexual. This tickled her escort. Auntie Harriett, who in a previous life played tackle for the Cleveland Browns football team, and had a rather sonorous voice, blasted out a loud "HA!" The entire restaurant, including the waiter and piano player, erupted. The laughter was sustained for the remainder of the evening.

In second place of my favorite memories was a shopping excursion with my friend Carol. Carol was a NYC dominatrix, and had an off-color albeit very funny sense of humor. A rustic store called 'Marine Specialties' was P-town's version of an Army-Navy store. It was a knickknack lover's paradise. It had everything, from hurricane candles, signal flags from the 19th century, anchor chains, 19th century clothing, ancient uniforms, an old navy diver's suit, it even had a World War One torpedo. The moment we entered the store and started exploring, Carol started talking about how she could use every item we found. We hadn't gotten 20 feet into the store before we were laughing so hard we couldn't move, then we found the torpedo. That did it. I was laugh ing so hard I had to use the display cases to hold myself up. I never had so much fun shopping in my life.

According to the letters from participants I received, my favorite memory was everybody else's favorite memory as well. We were having our usual party on the second floor of the Crown & Anchor. Everyone was there and ready to party. Dorothy, who had given us such a beautiful tribute to Frances at the '82 FanFair Follies, had a new character she wanted to introduce. She asked me to come and escort her to the party. Her character was a cockney dowager tosspot named Mrs. Shufflewick. She carried a crocheted bag containing her bottle of gin. I took her by her arm for she was clearly unsteady, then escorted her to the party where she launched into a carefully prepared routine which had everyone cramped with laughter. Her story contained such passages as when she went home, thought she would surprise her husband and got undressed, tiptoed upstairs only to find herself naked on the top deck of a cross-town bus, and of the time when she was being pursued by a war veteran tossing his pension book in the air like there was no tomorrow. The old vet pursued Mrs. Shufflewick into an alley where she was trapped, with one foot in a dustbin the other in an ashcan, saying, "This is it tonight Gladys, death or dishonor. Well I bloody well wasn't going to die tonight!"

Those of us who witnessed this performance were laughing so hard we had tears in our eyes, and our sides hurt. Carol, sitting on the bed which was mobbed with people, including me, was laughing so hard she bounced up and down, until the bed collapsed, and she found herself at the bottom of a tangled mass of people, which included me. Even Mrs. Shufflewick started laughing. It was a performance none of us would ever forget.

The outing was successful, and a lot of fun. However, as with every event with which I was involved, when it ended I was exhausted. I needed some quiet time to reflect on the event, and get refocused. It was important that I never forget what I was doing and why I was doing it, which was to build a community. To me parties were trivial, good for fun and friendship, but not much else. To me what was important at the outing was the way old-timers helped new-timers feel welcome and never feel alone, Also, what was important was meeting and sharing ideas with people who were leaders in their own areas, people such as Bebe from New York City, Susan from Canada, Ellen and Dorothy from the Pacific Northwest, Kim from Colorado, Elaine from Michigan, and Harriet from Connecticut.

In Provincetown my way of getting refocused and mellow was to sneak away by myself, Hike out to Long Point and walk the beaches, or climb the Pilgrim Monument, feel the wind, smell the salt air blowing in from the ocean, to regenerate and to think.

The rest of 1983 went something like this: I was compiling the Tapestry out of my bedroom, which meant I rarely got out of my cave and was working on it alone. The Tapestry was turning into a monster. Next came the July 4th pool party. The August Clam Bake, then our annual chicken BBQ. What a job that was.   My October schedule was 10/7-9 out to P-town for Lee Brewster's weekend. 10/14, back to P-town for Fantasia Fair. 10/16 back to P-town for the leader's meeting. 10/18 back to P-town for a guild meeting. 10/21 back to P-town for a business dinner. Back to Wayland for our Halloween Party which as always was a prodigious undertaking, coordinating the Fall clean-up, then Thanksgiving dinner for 35+ people in our tiny little home.   Finally, fin ishing the year with a Christmas party, and the awards banquet. Then it was on to 1984, and get ready to do it all again.

In 1983, Tiffany saw the formation of two new support Groups. Carol founded a support group for wives, and Rachia founded a support group for transsexuals. The house was being used for what we bought it for in the first place, to serve our community and those affected by our community, and it really pleased me to see our people pitching in. The Tiffany Club was growing and becoming effective, and the Tapestry kept on getting bigger.

1984 was a very sad year, and a time of personal crisis for me. It was sad because the AIDS pandemic hit Provincetown, and took a terrible toll. I first became acquainted with AIDS when it took the life of someone I knew. That person was a sexually promiscuous prostitute, and not particularly pleasant. Like most people I shrugged my shoulders, and went about my business. I remember feeling a sense of indifference towards the victim, and feeling anger towards people who claimed AIDS was God's way of punishing gay people. One thing I did not feel was concern. Then I heard Lynne Carter, a long-time entertainer, resident of Provincetown, and owner of the Pilgrim House Where Fantasia Fair held so many of its functions, had died. Then I became concerned.

Lynne was a friend, and had gone out of his way to accommodate the Fair, and to help our people feel welcome in P-town. I remembered him scolding me for calling him a female impersonator. He was a professional female "impressionist" after all. He considered impersonators too often played cruelty for laughs. He was never cruel, and mimicked life. Among his credits he was the first female "impressionist" to play Carnegie Hall. He moved to Provincetown and bought the Pilgrim House, where I made his acquaintance.

Brandie Alexander and Tiffany Jones both died, and AIDS moved from being a concern to become a real threat. Brandie was beautiful, and a wonderful entertainer. She was entertaining in P-town during the first Fantasia Fair, and befriended the Fair participants. Because of her efforts, the Fair became a most memorable experience, and was voted 'Miss Most Helpful'.

I sincerely liked her, both as an entertainer, and as a person.

Tiffany Jones was also an entertainer in P-town. She had named herself 'Tiffany Jones the Texas Tornado' after a cartoon character she saw on a milk carton. The first time I saw her she was dressed as a nun on a pair of roller skates performing 'The Vatican Rag'. She was wonderful. She was a terrific entertainer, proud of her profession, and that underneath it all she was still a man. She finished each show by stripping of her costume and by singing a song from the stage show 'La Cage Au Folle', "What Makes A Man A Man".

"I know my life is not a crime. I'm just a victim of my time. I stand defenseless. Nobody has the right to judge what is right for me. Tell me if you can, what makes a man a man?"

Ernest Dugas, the manager of the Gifford House, who had made such an exceptional effort on our behalf, and had become a staunch friend, died. Preston Babbitt, owner of the Rose and Crown guest house, and my hairdresser and friend, died. The list went on and on. It seemed like the entire population of P-town was dying. It was very frightening. What an empty helpless feeling.

History part 15

AIDS was by no means limited to P-town. I heard my friend Diane, and several other members of Mayflower had succumbed. To make matters worse, our own Laura had been found beaten to death, her body stuffed into the trunk of a car, and discarded into the Charles River. That put the entire Tiffany Club and all those who attended our functions in danger. If Laura could wind up murdered, so could the rest of us. Death and violence had come too close to home, and there was nothing I could do about it.

I wasn't particularly worried about the Wives' Group, their idea of an exciting time was to get dolled up and go out to dinner. I was more worried about our parties. We were attracting over 100 people to each event. We were on good relations with our neighbors and with the town authorities, but we were also well enough known that there was no telling what bigots and kooks we could attract. I was particularly worried about my kids on the Sewer Tour, people whose idea of excitement was to get dolled up and hit the seedy bars. That's what Laura did, and she wound up dead.

On a personal note, beside being worried about the well-being of my people, I was in my tenth year of serving the transgender community, had burned up my personal resources, was losing my health, was being attacked for my tardiness with the Tapestry and for my financial management of Tiffany, the Tapestry, and our functions, and was being accused of being power hungry and trying to make money off the community. I was also being attacked for being transsexual and not a cross-dresser, which to me was pure bigotry. I was emotionally and spiritually fried, and wanted out.

Unfortunately, I had no place to go. I owned the house, and couldn't in good conscience kick everybody out and sell it. We had come too far for that. I couldn't go back to the mountains. I was way too far out of shape, and I had lost my contacts. Thinking about creating a resume' gave me nightmares. My work history? Well, I was a life guard, and in three years I managed to save a beach ball, a boxer dog which beat me back to shore, and an orange crate. I was an academic bum for eight years, and wound up with a degree in philosophy, perhaps the most worthless degree imaginable. I was a ski bum for eleven years, with no other responsibility than to teach people how to slide down a hill without killing themselves. I worked three years for the Appalachian Mountain Club, which involved a t of backpacking and escorting a lot of Happy-Appies around the hills looking for mushrooms and interesting plants. I did run the ridges for a while, and managed to carry a few wounded or frost-bitten souls off the mountain. I even managed to dig a few gaboons (garbage dumps), but I didn't think anyone scanning my resume' would be impressed with that. I worked some with the Forest Service, but the Forest Service wanted me to either be a cop or empty garbage cans. I would have been the worst cop imaginable, and wasn't really into maintaining the cleanliness of camp sites or picnic areas. I did some construction work but couldn't stand the phony macho atmosphere, and was far too inclined to tell the boss what he could go do with himself. I held various jobs in sales, but hated the game of foisting an unwanted and unneeded product on somebody just to get their money. I could possibly have gone back and try to become a teacher, but had no idea what I could teach, certainly not the three R's. Teaching Logical Fallacies or Metaphysics were not valid options. My writing and editorial skills were limited to the Tapestry.

I had no mind or heart for business. The only time I was self-motivated to accomplish anything was when I began working on behalf of the transgender community. I couldn't see any place in the world for me. That left me with the Tiffany Club, but my dreams had faded, and I was crispy crusted burn-out. That meant continuing what I no longer wanted to do, pursuing my dreams and effort for nothing, and being punished for my efforts. There was nothing left but the reality of being burned out, without future options.   In 1984 my life looked grim.

To top it all off, at the 1983 Fan/Fair leaders' conference I was given a mandate to coordinate the 1984 leaders' conference during Tiffany's spring outing.   Unfortunately, many of the leaders who gave me that mandate were going to be involved with conferences of their own, such as 'the Phi Chapter's Rites of Spring', Joyce Dewhurst's 'Poconos Weekend', the Outreach Institute's symposium with AASECT/SSSS (professional organizations for educators, counselors and therapists), the Midwest organizations' 'Be All You Can Be', 'Shangri-La West', and so on.   These events were all happening at the same time, which meant the leaders who gave me the mandate knew at the time they would not be attending, thereby guaranteeing failure.   Homicide was an option.

To their credit, when the leaders' conference did happen, Ariadne Kane, Virginia Prince, Susan Huxford (Canada), and many members from the Tiffany Club were in attendance. Even with limited attendance, we still managed to accomplish a great deal, such as laying the groundwork for developing and international organization, a proposed constitution for that organization, and how to make it happen.   In spite of the guaranteed failure, we did not fail.

History part 16

Despite being in a dark depression and a crispy crusted burn-out,1984 did present me with flickers of hope.   All of our functions kept getting better and bigger.   We were learning how to coordinate these functions to the best benefit of the participants.   I was attending at least one other convention a month in places such as Syracuse, New York City, Philadelphia, Chicago, Denver, Kansas City, Pajaro Dunes California, Cincinnati and the universally popular Province town. It seemed like I was everywhere, but I was doing a great deal of networking. I also did a lot of coffee drinking with folks, talking about mutual support, cooperation and the dream of an actual, active and effective world-wide community. Working together for the benefit of all, Symbiotic Synergism. This travelling and talking helped me meet with and build a mutual support system with groups from around the country and Canada, and from foreign countries, such as the Beaumont Society of England, TRANS-CCL of France, the Elizabeth Club of Japan, the Seahorse Club of Australia and Hedesthia of New Zealand.

The objective was to create a community, and that was what I was trying to do, to create a common bond and communication and empowerment that would bring all niches of our community together, to work together for the benefit of all.

Although I thought our leadership conference was guaranteed to fail, it was very productive, and laid the path for and shed light on future projects. We were even making positive contact with incarcerated cross-dressers and transsexuals. One, a transsexual who had prostituted herself to pay for surgery, was on death row for murdering a customer because he had threatened her life. (That brought back memories of Laura. Laura's murderer was never caught. I wondered if the customer had succeeded in murdering the transsexual, would he have been on death row? It was clear we had a lot of work to do in the areas of public safety, the law, politics and justice.) We also had a growing gaggle of lawyers and rabble rousers ready to do the work.

The objective was to build a community. Political and social activists, and gender friendly lawyers fighting for human rights were an important niche in that community. Another arena that offered a flicker of hope was among the professionals. The researchers were taking us seriously, and were no longer addressing us with a "Me doctor, you patient" attitude. Leaders in this group were Doctor Roger Peo, a member of the Harry Benjamin International Gender Dysphoria Association (HBIGDA), the Society for Scientific Study of Sex (SSSS) and a member of the Tiffany Club Board of Directors, members of American Association of Sexual Educators Counselors and Therapists (AASECT), Doctor Vern L. Bullough of New York State University-Buffalo and Doctor Richard F. Docter of California State University-Northridge. Ariadne Kane and the Outreach Institute was also doing considerable networking with the professional community.

The objective was to build a community. Educators, researchers, therapists, psychologists, medical doctors, psychiatrists, all helping professionals were another important niche in that community.

My favorite flicker of hope emerged from our own Wives Support Group. Carol Diamond and Bobbie Chandler had done an excellent job coordinating the Tiffany Club Wives Group and developed a considerable network of couples from around the nation. They had organized a couples outing in Provincetown for the first weekend of October. They marketed the outing for "committed couples". That pleased me because they did not market to couples based on sexual orientation or gender identity. They didn't even discriminate against couples of the same sex. It was an event for couples where the only requirement was the couple was in a committed relationship, a policy which was completely nondiscriminatory. I loved that. I loved it even more because the wives, a group which had traditionally been ignored, were taking the lead. I just wish Sherry had lived to see it. I was sure she would have loved it too.

The objective was to create a community that would serve all niches of that community. Wives and partners were defi nitely an important niche of that community. The leadership for that niche had to come from within that niche, and that is what Carol and Bobbie did.

As a courtesy, I was invited to attend the function, despite not being in a committed relationship. It was an invitation I was pleased to accept. The organizers had reserved the Ocean's Inn in P-town, one of my very favorite guest houses, and home to one of the best restaurants in town. The stipulation for my participation was that I respect that the Inn was for the couples, so I took a room at the 12 Carver Guest House, which was just around the corner.

Fortunately for me, Cheryl Costa, a sister pre-op transsexual, was in attendance with her wife Karyn, so I was not completely alone and out of place. The kids, like most everyone I had met, had a wonderful time in P-town, great end-of-the-season shopping, exploring P-town's countless hide-aways, renewing old friendships, fine dining, gorgeous views, whale watching excursions, and my traditional hikes to Long's Point Lighthouse, and a mandatory visit to the Pilgrim museum and Monument.

The most memorable event of the outing happened during one of our traditional pajama parties. The most memorable events always seemed to happen during our late night parties. We were gathered in Helen and Sydney's room. I brought my guitar, and found that Karyn had a beautiful singing voice, which offered fine opportunities for harmony.

As the night rolled on our spirits were lifted, and kept getting higher. Finally, at about 4:00 o'clock in the morning, we were about to get into a rousing version of 'Mama Don't Allow', when there was a crash against the window screen, and a horrible stench of dead fish wafted across the room. A fisherman who lived in his house behind the Inn threw his bait bucket at us, followed by a loud contemptuous "Shut the F**K up!" We had kept the poor guy up all night and it was time for him to go to work. Needless to say we were profoundly apologetic, but the stench remained. We all slinked off to bed leaving Helen and Sydney to deal with it.

While in college during the Viet Nam war, participating in anti-war demonstrations, I had eggs thrown at me. I never had bait thrown at me. After the incident I could truthfully say, "I have been egged, and now I have been dead fished."

Another incident occurred during Halloween. Betsy Shaw, a fixture in the northeast transgender community, a founding mother of the Gamma Chapter and the Cherrystone Club, and a member of Tiffany's board of directors, was sponsoring a Halloween party. My friend Pat and I were going to attend. We had just welcomed a new couple, Anne and Siobhan (add cherry stone 4493?) Donovan, and invited them to come with us. We gave them directions to Betsy's, which were complicated to say the least, and invited them to follow us. Somewhere along the way we lost them, and assumed they returned home. When we arrived at Betsy's we found a number of old friends, and original members of the Gamma Chapter. One thing was obvious, this crew was well past caring about public images. Betsy, our hostess's costume was a flasher, complete with overcoat, naked legs et al. Anne and Siobhan showed up. Betsy greeted them at the door. Anne glanced at Betsy, her overcoat and naked legs, muttered a quiet, "My God, what have we gotten ourselves into?", turned a waxy white, and entered. Both Anne and Siobhan had a marvelous time, and all was well.

History part 17

Malinda Anderson, founder of LIPS, Lambchops International Preservation Society, announced she was organizing a new group, the T-TVC, the Tired TV Club. It was a joke, but a joke that came to me at exactly the right time. Malinda exclaimed, "Dressing up was once a thrill, an adventure. But, the truth is, cross-dressing is JUST PLAIN WORK! Instead of the gawd-awful amount of time I've spent getting dressed I could have had a beer or studied the Peloponnesian Wars. Then after an evening of prancing around the bars I feel like the oldest Tart in Soho. It's time we tired TVs came out of the closet." For me cross-dressing wasn't the issue, but the frustration, the work, the criticism the loss of my vision and sense of purpose made me a haggard deep fried burn-out. The thought of a support for burn-outs like me was very appealing, so I immediately became a charter member.

Then something wonderful happened to help rejuvenate my spirit. One of our Tiffany members, Roberta Dearborn, co-ordinated a fund-raising campaign for Children's Hospital. The Tiffany Club was engaging in a project to benefit the public good. This surpassed even my expectations. What an extraordinary way to build a bridge between ourselves and the public. Roberta acquired a substantial sum by auctioning off a cabbage patch kid named 'Jilly'. In 1984 a cabbage patch kid was a treasure. The VP of Public Affairs for the Children's Hospital sent the Tiffany Club a formal letter of appreciation. This unprecedented effort had the potential for the public to validate the existence of our community and opened the door to exciting new potentials.

At the same time we became aware that silicone injections were a primary source of kidney failure. That placed a significant number of our community at risk, and the Tapestry was a primary way to alert our community of the danger.
Also, the Tapestry became a primary source of critical information written by medical doctors, researchers, and helping professionals. The Tapestry took on a new importance, and it was my responsibility to publish the Tapestry. That meant

in spite of being worn out, my work was more important than my trivial debilitation.

For quite some time I had been receiving letters and articles on religion. "God said this, God did that, God made this and that," "Why did God make me this way?" Etc. My experience in the Pemigewasset Wilderness was to me a religious experience, rather a spiritual revelation, so to the chagrin of many, I entered the fray. I wrote an article concluding once we've cut through the human ego and the balderdash, we are not so far apart. To my surprise I created a firestorm worldwide. I heard from priests, nuns, ministers and religious people of every ilk. I even heard from several psychologists and one psychiatrist. Their comments were nearly unanimously favorable. It wasn't that I was rattling anybody's theological cage, but I was clarifying how a person's faith might work for them, open the door for communication and find the common ground. Here are a few things I said:

"I am a spiritual but not a religious person, and have a profound respect for Nature." "...God is Nature, the unification of all the qualities of Nature; Oneness!" "Nature is not to be worshiped or feared, it is to be loved and respected." "Nature is not a concept, label or value judgment created from the imagination of man." "Language is in the realm of the intellectual. Nature transcends the intellectual. Language is not a quality of Nature."

"Purpose, Meaning and reason-for-being are concepts, not qualities of Nature and therefore not qualities of God." "No one and no thing exists for a reason. It exists because it exists. It is Man's responsibility to assign meaning. "Masculinity and femininity are gender assignments, not qualities of Nature, and therefore not qualities of God. It is Man's responsibility to define masculine and feminine

"Right, wrong, good, bad, sin, beauty, ugly, etc. are value judgments, not qualities of Nature, and therefore not qualities of God. It is Man's responsibility to define 'right and wrong', 'good and bad', 'sin', 'beauty', etc."

"Superiority and inferiority are value judgments, concepts created from Man's ego, not qualities of Nature, and therefore not qualities of God."

"The qualities that make Man also make the Universe. Man is a manifestation of Nature, and therefore a manifestation of God, as are all things that exist."

"It is the absolute height of human arrogance to believe Man has the divine right to exploit and destroy. Nature, God, creates, maintains and destroys in a never-ending harmonious cycle of existence. Man has the greatest power to destroy that cycle. Therefore, Man has the greatest responsibility to not destroy that cycle. Man is the caretaker of existence, and has the responsibility to live in balance with that never-ending harmonious cycle of existence. Man has the responsibility to live in harmony with Nature, with God and with himself. Man's REASON FOR BEING is to serve as caretaker of this earth and of each other."

"We cannot live in harmony with ourselves, much less Nature, God, if we live in accordance with an artificially consigned gender, in conflict with our spirits."

"To say cross-dressing or being transsexual is wrong makes absolutely no sense. To say these phenomena are wrong, is wrong." "Cross-dressing can be a very powerful sensual experience. It can be a religious experience, a way to 'feel' Nature, God. Nonsense you say? Think about it. Actually, don't think about it, experience it!"

"Anyone who has cross-dressed and felt tears of joy, has had a religious experience. Anyone who has hoisted an ax, felt sweat drip from their palms and brow, and felt a happy anger explode from their soul as the log split from the power of their blow, has had a religious experience. Anyone who has felt the wind rustle through their skirt and caress silky smooth legs, or felt the poetry of a gentle flowing gait, has had a religious experience. Anyone who has touched a flower, felt its beauty, allowed its essence to touch his soul, has had a religious experience. Life itself is a religious experience that cannot be explained, only experienced."

"The urge to cross-dress or to be transsexually inclined does not mean you are in disharmony with Nature, God. If you do not realize this, you will never achieve peace-of-mind, or achieve harmony with Nature, God."

"Love and hate, harmony and disharmony exist, but I have the power to choose. Love works better than hate, so I choose love. Harmony works better than disharmony, so I choose harmony. To love and live in harmony with myself, and Nature, God, is the cornerstone of my existence. It is also the cornerstone of most religions. As I said, once we've cut through the ego and the balderdash, we are not that far apart. Love and Happiness to you all!"

History part 18

(Did I screw up? Hit send message instead of save draft. My bad. Sorry.)

My article on religion was an important piece for me to write, because it reminded me I had a reason for being that transcended exhaustion, and that was to be a caretaker for our people, and to build a community of caretakers for our people. I had a reason for being and that was enough to keep me going. However, I was also aware that being motivated by a reason for being was going to be in conflict with people who were motivated by money and power, which was almost everyone I knew.   It made for an ugly but necessary future.

I had functions to run, things to do, and places to go.   One of those places was the Windy City's Spring Fling in Chicago which was to be held in Skokie IL from April 4 to the 7th.   I volunteered to drive Harriet Lane and a swarm of her folks to Chicago.   If I knew Harriet, and I did, I knew the party would have begun before I picked her up, and would continue until we reached Skokie.   If I thought I had a headache before, it would have been nothing like the headache I would have after an 18-hour drive with that crew, and especially since I was driving a Dodge Aries K, the most untrustworthy car I ever owned, all plastic and tin, and uncomfortable to boot.

Fortunately, we arrived in Skokie with relatively few incidents.   When we arrived my passengers, having had a few cat-naps along the way, bounced out of the car and were ready to party.   I hauled my bedraggled body out of the car, bleary eyed and wobbly, wearing a holey burgundy sweatshirt and ratty dungarees covered in ketchup and mustard stains (thanks to Burger King Whoppers while driving), appearing as ragged as I felt.   I also arrived with a proposal.   Before I presented that proposal, I had to get some sleep.

After I woke up, scraped off the mustard and ketchup, climbed into my best business drag, and entered the fray to lobby for my proposal.   I managed to meet lots of folks who were supportive of my proposal, and a few who in time would become working partners.   Most notably among these was Yvonne Cook from Indiana.   She was tall, thin, with lots of freckles and a strawberry mop of hair.   She couldn't have been more Scottish if she tried.   She was also filled with an intense desire to accomplish something, a fire of enthusiasm. She reminded me of me, or at least the way I was before

Iburned out. Yvonne renewed my spirit and revived old dreams. I liked her immediately.

One thing I learned over the years was if there was work to be one, especially creative work, it was best done over food or beer, or at least, coffee. My friend Ellen Summers from Oregon was in attendance, bringing back memories of our lunch on the top deck of the Crown and Anchor, when we were discussing the future of our community while picking hailstones out of our lobster rolls. This time we just shared coffee. I had never seen one human being drink so much coffee. As usual our conversations were about ideas and how to make those ideas come true. I also shared a lot of food with Bette Johnson from Texas. I met Bette at the previous year's Tiffany's Spring Outing. She clearly had a great time, but seemed she would have been more at home in a Board Room. Most of our kids would walk the streets of P-town inappropriately dressed in cocktail dresses. Bette walked the streets inappropriately dressed in a business suit. She had a business sense, but she also had a grasp of our vision and an opportunity to pitch in, which was an excellent combination.

History part 19

We called for a leaders' meeting Sunday morning. That would provide me with an opportunity to formally present my proposal. We had a good crowd of attendees, including Yvonne, Bette and Ellen. We had a nice continental breakfast and plenty of coffee and fruit juice. Ellen had her own private urn of coffee and a large box of donuts. As I said earlier, I had never seen a human being drink so much coffee or eat so many donuts

"This was my proposal".

The Tiffany Club was not created to be a local support group. It was a project created to serve our whole community. The Tapestry was created as the publications arm of that project, and also created to serve and unify our whole community. It was designed for growth. We achieved a functional constitution which listed 'conventions' as one of its services, and obtained 501 C 3, tax exempt status. Several years ago we created a leadership conference which was first held at Fantasia Fair, then transferred to the Tiffany Club's Spring Outing. At the last meeting we established the template for the formation of an international organization serving the entire community and those who affected and were affected by our community. That organization was called the International Foundation for Gender Education (IFGE). It was time we built on all that and created a Community Convention, a Movers and Shakers convention, sponsored by and coordinated by IFGE, which was tax exempt and designed to serve everyone.

The Tiffany Club could form a separate educational branch (as the Tapestry was a separate publications branch). We could build on Tiffany's constitution and tax exempt status to bring the International Foundation for Gender Education (IFGE) into fruition. IFGE would then sponsor this new convention on behalf of the entire community and publish the Tapestry. Using the convention and the Tapestry as a base, IFGE would have unlimited potential to build and serve our community.

The proposal had general approval, and we spent the rest of the morning chatting about how to make it happen. After the meeting I spent my time trying to drum up support for the proposal. When I arrived home I had a sad surprise. It was an old problem, and not really a surprise. A small group of Tiffany's Board of Directors was determined to prevent the Tiffany Club from being involved. I didn't understand their problem, but then I never did understand. To me it was shallow, short sighted and destructive thinking. It was the same attitude I had faced when no one would sign the lease for Cherrystone's apartment, the attitude that nearly prevented Tiffany from being born, that killed NACD, that dropped the workload of Tiffany, Tiffany's functions, the Tapestry, etc. on me. It was the attitude of people not wanting to pitch in, and not wanting others to do so either. I was so sick of that self-centered obstructionist "To hell with anyone else," shit. I could see what was coming. Eventually the Tiffany Club and IFGE would have to go their separate ways, to the detriment of both groups.

I thought it was understood that Tiffany was created to build a community and to serve all our people. Tiffany was the means to create a cadre of like-minded people who shared the vision and to work together to make it happen. The creation of an educational branch called IFGE was a natural step in that process. The only thing I could do was to ignore these obstructionists and keep working. Whatever was going on it was an unfortunate mess

Two Hands

One of Merissa Sherrill Lynn's earliest trademarks was the two hands holding a rose bud. One hand with a diamond bracelet the other a man hand. The rose bud signified the beauty of trans-life with both the thorns and a fragrance to delight the senses.

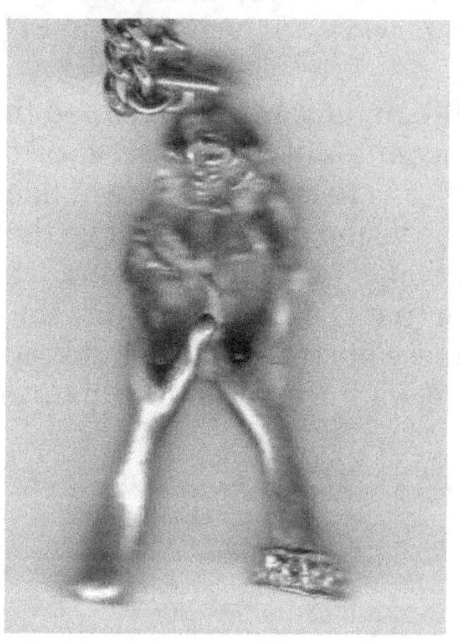

The male is embracing the female, the female cradling the male and the rose. Used as a signature for the International Foundation for Gender Education (IFGE) this symbol spoke to all who felt the unity and the connectives of gender diversification.

Originally only a few were cast in silver with several holding a small diamond chip in the rose bud. These symbols were available only from the IFGE offices in very limited supplies and today are treasured keepsakes from that time.

After my encounter with this small group of miscreants I was introduced to an unfamiliar bundle of sensations. In the past when I encountered obstructionists, I felt sad, frustrated and ready to toss it all in and head back to the mountains. This time I felt betrayed, disappointed and angry. Anger was a new sensation for me and I didn't really know how to handle it. I thought everyone understood what we were trying to do, and just did not understand why anyone would disagree. Anger was not a very productive sensation, so I ignored them.   It was important I focused on the convention and on IFGE.

We were trying to build a community. That meant caring about each other and taking care of each other. It Meant Symbiotic Synergism, working together for the benefit of all. Local social clubs filled one little niche of that community, it did not mean creating a small social club and stopping there.

It was quite some time before I understood what all the falderal was about. It was a basic lack of communications. When I created IFGE, put it under Tiffany's tax exempt status and had IFGE take over publication of the Tapestry, they thought I had dissolved the Tiffany Club. Their actions were based on how they could save Tiffany.

The Tiffany Club was created to be a basic tool in the creation of a community. The Tapestry was also a tool to be of service to that community. The Tiffany Club was intended to attract a cadre of like-minded people who would work together for the benefit of all. IFGE would come under the auspices of Tiffany as the educational division of Tiffany. The true advantages of this arrangement were Tiffany could continue to be a dynamic local organization, IFGE could be a dynamic international organization, and still work together for the benefit of all.   Also, IFGE's Board of Directors could come from the local area thereby eliminating a communications problem we would have with Board members coming from to-hell-and-gone, and being able to work together only on scattered occasions. With this arrangement IFGE could function effectively, while bringing together organizational representatives from all over the world which would create a broad-based community-wide cadre of leaders. With this arrangement we would in fact become a community.

With the Tiffany Club going its own way, the whole project was in danger. With the Tiffany Club gone my core support was gone. Being alone with a project like IFGE ahead of me was a frightening proposition. There was nothing to do but to do it, but it did mean I had to pretty much start over.

The next meeting for the convention was to be held at the 1985 'Be All You Want To Be' conference to be held in Ann Arbor Michigan the week after Tiffany's P-town outing. Besides dealing with the day-to-day work for Tiffany and preparing for P-town, I was busy. I contacted every organization selling the idea of the convention, looking for representatives to serve on the board of advisors and setting up basic business stuff for IFGE such as checking accounts. By the time 'Be All' arrived, most everything was in place. At 'Be All' we had representatives from 26 organizations, set the date for our convention for March 1987, the location in Chicago, and Elaine Willey and I were selected co-coordinators.

During the 1986 Windy City Spring Fling it was time to go hotel hunting for the first Coming Together convention. It was important we find a hotel that reflected an attitude of pride, self-respect and dignity. If our kids could walk around cross-dressed in a first class hotel, they could not help but feel first class. Yvonne Cook and I had the honors. We visited hotels all around Chicago. Most of the hotels, including the Sheraton, the Marriott, and the Hilton didn't even want to talk to us. We finally arrived at the Ramada, an 800-room monster near the Chicago O'Hare airport. We were escorted around and found everything we needed, including a French restaurant that boasted Cary Grant as a regular customer. We were treated to dinner at the French restaurant, and received a lengthy narration of the hotel's more notorious moments. We contracted our first convention for March 4-9, 1987.

History part 21

In 1986 Mariette joined our team. Mariette Pathy Allen was a professional photographer for New York City, and had been a treasured friend of our community for many years. Mariette was compiling a collection of photos of members of our community, and writing bios for a book she was developing she called "Transformations". It was a book she hoped to have published before our 1988 convention. It was to be the most tasteful and dignified publication concerning our community in existence.

Mariette asked me for an interview, which I gleefully granted. We were sitting at Mariette's dining table when she placed her recorder on the table. To test it out we started singing. We had a harmony that was quite nice. When we were done, I said, "That was beautiful." However, when we played it back we heard the most bloody awful caterwauling imaginable. We sounded like two really drunk cows standing on our udders. It was truly terrible. Then we heard, "That was beautiful," we exploded. For years Mariette and I couldn't look at each other without remembering that incredible sound and bursting into laughter. Mariette came to Wayland to take a portrait for her book. We went outside for early morning light. I was still in my nightgown. The grass and day lilies were damp with dew and reflected the sunlight. It was quiet and serine, and I was laughing myself silly thinking about that recording. I was laughing so hard I was crying, and that's the picture Mariette chose for her book. At our 1991 convention in Denver, the Rocky Mountain News chose that picture for a full page spread on the convention. I was immortalized wearing my nightie surrounded by a bunch of wet flowers, in a fit of hysterics. If the objective was to present me in a proud and dignified manner, she could have chosen a more august picture

For the first portrait cover of the Tapestry we chose Mariette's beautiful portrait of Pam Van Buren, an active member of our community. If the Tapestry was to be an effective instrument to promote pride and self-respect, we couldn't have picked a better exemplar than Pam. Pam was classy and dignified, a superb representative for the community and for our journal.

The Tapestry was a tool to present ourselves to ourselves, and to the world, in a good and positive way. It was also a tool for information, education and unifying our community. For these reasons I wanted to use the cover to introduce our community's leaders, and to tell their stories. I was afraid the Tapestry might be used to satisfy somebody's vanity, or political action or to make money without actually making a positive contribution to our community. I was afraid IFGE might evolve in the same way. The purpose of Tiffany, the IFGE and the Tapestry was to build a community in a good way. That meant pretty pictures, political action and money weren't good enough. Mariette's photography and her connections with our community would be a wonderful way avoid the nonsense and trivia and keep the focus on fulfilling our purpose.

Meanwhile, the work for the upcoming Tiffany '86 Outing, and the IFGE convention continued. It was time to gather the troops and head out to P-town for Tiffany's '86 Outing. It always did my spirit good to roll down route 6, see the Pil grim Monument rise in the distance, pass the summer homes neatly tucked away in the dunes, and pass the row of little white cottages before pulling into the Crown & Anchor's tiny little parking lot.

History part 22

The '86 Outing began in a unique way. We knew we were going to have a large turn-out, and a number of Tiffany members volunteered to pitch in. One of these volunteers was Jackie McDonald. Several years earlier I interviewed Jackie for Tiffany membership. I tried to make her feel as comfortable as possible, and make sure all was well, then escorted her to Tiffany. When I got there I turned around and Jackie was gone. At first I thought I had done to Jackie what Kay had done to me when I first came out. She left me stranded. Eventually Jackie called back, and I went and got her. She had just chickened out. If anyone knew how important it was to help newcomers feel welcome, it was Jackie.

Jackie had volunteered to be a hostess. We were expecting a newcomer from New Jersey, named Meagan. When Meagan came through the door, Jackie went to greet her. When their eyes met, both of them stood in frozen terror, then both spoke simultaneously, "What are YOU doing here?" It turned out Meagan was Jackie's brother, and neither one knew the other was a cross-dresser. As the Outing went on, naturally they took every opportunity to have their pictures taken, starting with the sign for the C&A's stage show 'Birds of a Feather', then on to a local restaurant 'The Painted Lady', but their favorite target was the poor guy dressed in the lobster suit in front of the Lobster Pot Restaurant. The lobster guy seemed to be the favorite of the Outing's character, Crazy

Shirley, Shirley K. from Pueblo Colorado. Shirley loved having a good time and pushing the limits. To me pushing the limits was good, albeit embarrassing. The further the limits got pushed, eventually there would be no limits, after which our community would become a fully integrated segment of society. The only problem was we had classless people who pushed the limits for no other reason than for the fun of pushing the limits, for no positive effect. There was a line which could be crossed, and even though Shirley pushed it she did not cross it, and for that reason she was a credit to our community. Besides that, she was fun.

My favorite moment with her was at dinner in the Lobster Pot. It was 25 years after Thalidomide, a sedative that caused birth defects, hit the market. At dinner we had wine served in small carafes. Shirley mentioned that the carafes looked like thalidomide babies. From then on the carafes were referred to as thalidomide carafes. For some really bad reason that struck us funny. We spent the rest of the night in a fit of giggles, ignoring the snickers and stares of the other patrons, making complete boobs of ourselves.

As with every Outing, we had an orientation. We invited a representative from the Police Department and two representatives from the P-town Business Guild representing over 200 businesses. For old-timers like me having the police assuring our safety and the business guild publicly soliciting our business, was normal. However for our newcomer's declaration of police protection and businesses openly welcoming us was definitely not normal, and was a bit bewildering. As I looked at the expressions of our first-timers, I could not help but think of how beautiful the world would be if it were as accepting and tolerant as P-town. I also asked, "Why wasn't it?" And, "What would we, as a community, have to do to remedy the situation?" The answer was to just keep doing what we were doing, until police protection and acceptance was normal for everyone.

Legal protection everywhere; tolerance, especially tolerance for each other, respect, especially self-respect, and acceptance, especially self-acceptance. Tolerance, respect, and acceptance as well as dignity and pride were all qualities we absolutely had to have if we absolutely had to have if we were to have any hope of working together for the benefit of all, or to build a community. For three days at Tiffany's Outing we talked about it, and how to implement it at IFGE's convention. We also talked about marketing the convention, logistics, financing, and all the nitty gritty of running an effective and successful convention. There was one tiny little oversight. The only program we planned for was a banquet honoring Virginia Prince. We had no programs. When we printed our brochure we overcame this oversight by saying, "Morning or Afternoon workshops." We never told anybody what those fantasy workshops were.

Of all the conventions, conferences and outing I coordinated or simply participated in, the first IFGE Convention was my favorite. My objective was to tap into the souls of our people, bring them together and build a community. We did it. In 1973 I entered the Pemigewasset Wilderness with an intense desire to be female and thoughts of suicide. When I emerged from the Wilderness I emerged with the awareness that being female was part of my being and that I had a feminine, gentle, loving and nurturing spirit.

I felt I could not have been given such beautiful gifts for no reason. I felt a need to use the gifts of my spirit in a good way, to work with all my sisters and brothers of the soul to make this a better world in which to live. For the first time in my life I felt as though my life had a purpose. From 1973 to 1987 my life was a long exercise in frustration and burn-out. The only thing that kept me from quitting was the sense that my life had meaning.   For the first time the IFGE Convention gave me the feeling that the gifts of my spirit were actually going to bear fruit.

By the time the Convention began, we had assembled quite a team. My co-director, Elaine willey, was a lovely lovely person, and a joy to work with. The coordinator, Bette Johnson, was a Texas business executive, intense and dynamic, a wellspring of knowledge and ideas, eager to make a difference, and to make it work.   We couldn't have found a better coordinator, or for that matter, a better boss. Our financial and vendors coordinator was Yvonne Cook, a lady on a crusade to correct past sins against our community, and to change the world for the better, and possessing the irrepressible energy of a hyper active border collie.   Our luncheons and banquet coordinator was Sheila Kirk, a lady of fervent dignity, who brought unsurpassed class to our events. Two of our real prizes were our audio-visual coordinator, Cheryl Powers, and our newsletter coordinator, Jamie McCloskey.

When we were planning the convention, we put out a call for our community's movers and shakers, and for people who wanted to become movers and shakers. When these folks came together, we had an explosion of enthusiasm and ideas. We didn't need any programs. We just brought everybody together and asked them what they wanted to do. If it weren't for our wonderful programs coordinators, Ellen Summers and Dorothy Finch, we would have had a dizzying cacophony of God-knows-what, but we wound up with a prodigious collection of ideas and moderators, who in truth when the sessions occurred were more like referees than moderators. We even wound up with special programs addressing transsexual issues, wives and significant others issues, and female-to-male issues

Cheryl choreographed and recorded every session, and made sure everyone who spoke could be heard, and the sessions could later be transcribed and recorded for history. Jamie and her daily bulletin was our primary means of communication. Without her no one would have known what was happening, what it was about, where it was happening, and who it was happening with. Without Jamie the whole convention would have disintegrated into chaos, but it didn't.

With the transcriptions from Cheryl's tapes, and the photography of Mariette Pathy Allen and Renee Chevalier, the convention became history, and everyone who attended made history.

History part 24

I could not have been more pleased and proud with the success of the convention. We laid an unbreakable foundation upon which the future of our community could be built. However, along with the evolution of the convention came immortal memories. For instance, Elaine and I arrived at the Ramada a week before the convention was to begin. We had no problems. The morning of the convention I received a phone call from a radio station called 'Murphy in the Morning.' After fourteen years of serving the transgender community, I had encountered my share of religious bigots, and ultra-right wing lightweights such as Rush Limbaugh, Morton Downey, and Boston's local nutcase, Howie Carr. When Murphy called, I wasn't surprised. Obviously, his objective was to give a good laugh to his listeners, at my expense.

His first question was, "Do I call you sir or madam?" I responded, "With me you have the security of knowing you can't go wrong." The technician in the background laughed. That laughter was heard on radios around Chicago.

He then wanted to know about my underwear, so I asked him if he interviewed everybody by asking them about their underwear. Again the guy in the background laughed. He asked me what I was wearing. I told him my sexiest dungarees and New England Patriots sweatshirt. The guy in the background laughed. Murphy was a Bears fan. He then commented, if he showed up at the Ramada, hee hee, would he see men running around in dresses? I told he was way too late for that, we had been there for a week.

The hotel management panicked. They thought the radio show would attract every bigot, neo-Nazi and skinhead in Chicago. Also, there was a convention for black Southern Baptists being held simultaneously in the hotel. It had the opposite effect. We did a landmark business with walk-ins, and information distribution. One distinguished businessman in a neat three-piece suit, was browsing our vendors, stuffing his briefcase with every goodie he could fit, when he was overheard saying, "I'm in heaven, and I can't do a damn thing about it."

The convention was held in Chicago, in the middle of winter. Naturally our participants brought their winter wardrobe. We had a heat wave, with temperatures in the 80's. The hotel was not prepared, so there was no air conditioning. There were a few people, such as Yvonne who had the metabolism of an alligator, who were very happy with the temperature, but the rest of us suffered.

When we were planning the convention, we tried to take everything into consideration. We were near the airport, we liked the spacious reception area, the meeting rooms, the restaurants, even the bar. They even gave us an entire concourse, concourse G, to ourselves. That meant we could have all the parties we wanted, without disturbing anyone. With a private entrance, it made it easy for folks to load and unload their cars. However, excluding the weather, there were a few things we overlooked. For instance, the hotel was huge, and concourse G was at one end and the meeting rooms were at the other. Yvonne, who was from Indiana, joked that she was almost home. Most of our attendees were men, men who were not used to wearing heels. It was an endurance just to go to breakfast. Besides walking around in a hotel hotter than a sauna, there were a lot of folks in considerable pain. There were also lots of folks wandering around the hotel barefooted.

Our first convention was beset with an abundance of characters. For instance, Helen, of P-town fame, had a copious supply of brass and fearlessness. When she learned there was a church group on the premises, the first thing she did was seek them out. At the end of the convention a prim elderly lady dressed in a lavender dress, came up to us and said in a rich Southern drawl, "When you first came I didn't know what to make of you, but y'all are the nicest folks." There where hugs all around, hugs thanks to Helen.

History part 25

Another unique personality was Naomi Owen. She was the president of the Chicago Chapter of Tri-Ess, co-founder and occasional director of the annual 'Be All You Can Be' conference, which was held alternately in Chicago, Detroit, Cleveland and Pittsburgh. She was also a newly elected member of IFGE's first Board of Directors. I had met Naomi the first time she came to Fantasia Fair. It was my duty to pick up people at the airport where I met her. She showed up with enough luggage to sink a battleship. She made a long forgotten joke, we shared a laugh, and had been friends ever since. She had a capricious sense of humor, and we never knew what she was going to say or do.

She came to an after-hours party with a bra that must have been a 54 DD. She had it fiber-glassed, and was using it as a chip-and-dip bowl. During the keynote luncheon which featured Virginia Prince as the primary speaker, Naomi stood up to introduce her. She produced a custom built three-cup bra for the mammary challenged among us, announced she had a few short comments and produced a scroll when unfurled went clear across the room. At the banquet honoring Virginia, Naomi stood up and presented her with a pair of gilded falsies.   She was large and jovial, and at each conference or meeting she would tell people everyone had an 'Aunt Rose' that looked like her. She was right.

Another character was Linda from Kentucky. She was tall and exotic, especially in her 6" stiletto heels, bold and brassy, and a bodacious flirt. I could understand why. She was married with a flock of kids, and owned a construction company. When else would she have the opportunity to be a bodacious flirt except at a transgender conference? It must have been extremely liberating for her. We all understood, because cross-dressing was extremely liberating for a great many people.

The hotel manager, fearing repercussions from the Murphy interview, arranged for a police presence at our functions. At one of our luncheons a diminutive policeman stood guard. Linda approached him. She towered over him, leaned down and I heard her softly say, "Hi there, big boy, can I see your gun?" He stood there terrified. Linda gave a quiet but truly wicked chuckle, and went on her way. I slapped my forehead, and said a silent, "Oh God!"

In another part of the hotel, the Pep Club for the Marquette University basketball team had gathered. Linda and Yvonne crashed the party. I never did find out what happened, but apparently they had a great time and there was no terminal fall-out. However, it did result in another slap on the forehead and a silent "oh God!"

Not all unique personalities were participants. One such personality was Jim Bridges. Jim was a Hollywood make-up artist with skills much needed and much in demand by many of our girls, me included. Jim's services and products kept him busy from the moment he arrived to the moment he left. I had an appointment. When I arrived, Jim, with hair blower in hand, was still busy with his previous client. He held the hair blower like a pistol, and remembering Linda's comment, I flippantly said, "Hi there big boy, can I feel your gun?"

Without a flinch, Jim responded, "That's not a gun, that's a Winchester!" We both laughed, and from then on, "Hi there big boy, can I feel your Winchester?" became a greeting and a perpetual private joke. Some years later, Jim presented me with a Winchester box filled with long-stem roses. Jim Bridges always had, and always will have, a warm spot in my heart.

Another professional friend at the convention was Niela Miller. Niela was the founder of People Systems Potential, a counseling service in Massachusetts. She was also a long-time presenter and friend of the Tiffany Club and Fantasia Fair. We were good friends through our mutual love of folk music. No convention was complete without a good sit-down sing along with Niela.

The Coming Together Convention was invented to create a community. A community meant working together for mutual benefit and mutual support. Mutual support meant peer support. Peer support had always been a problem. We tried to overcome it in the Tiffany Club with the creation of our hostess program. Still, people split into cliques and special interest groups.   Because of inadequate peer support true horror stories continued to pour in from around the world.   Niela came to the convention and conducted a special two-day workshop specifically on the issues of peer support.   The Workshop taught the leaders of our community how to do a better job of providing peer support.   It was one of the best received and most important programs at the convention.   Milesa Phar from the Crossroads group in Michigan summarized, "The most important job we have is to provide effective peer support, and to do that we must educate ourselves first."   Niela's workshop did just that.

History part 26

Some of the most elegant aspects of the convention were our luncheons and banquets.   Sheila Kirk, the luncheons coordinator, was an elegant lady and her functions reflected that. The reception featured a live harpist in the background, softly playing classical music, a lovely buffet, complete with server and carver, surrounding an ice sculpture of a swan.   It couldn't have been a more beautiful function, or better opportunity for folks to mix, to talk and to network.

At one luncheon the keynote speaker was Virginia Prince. Virginia always had an exasperating talent for tweaking my philosophical genes.   Virginia's history was based on serving the heterosexual male cross-dressers and their families.   To me this was a special interest group, just one niche in a rainbow of niches that made up or served our community. The convention was created to serve the entire community, our helping professionals, researchers, teachers, significant others, vendors and anyone else who had an interest in or affected our community.   The first three words of her speech made me cringe.   Virginia stood omnisciently at the lectern, looked over her audience, and began her speech with, "Hello my sisters! ..."   With three little words she separated herself from everyone, especially our female-to-male brothers, from our transsexual attendees, myself included, from everyone who did not identify as one of her heterosexual cross-dresser sisters.

I feared her speech would be antagonistic and divisive. It didn't turn out that way. It turned out to be a beautiful speech, one of the best I ever heard. At one point she asked, "Out of curiosity, how many in this audience, came out as a direct or indirect result of my efforts?" Fully three/quarters of the audience, myself included, raised their hands. I began to take notice when she made substantive comments like, "I see this convention as a kind of collimating lens - one that receives light coming in from many directions and putting it out all going in the same direction." And, "We have to find the common denominator ..." And, "We have to reduce the internal strife and polarization, and all of us face in the same direction and realize that the real antagonist is ignorance and misunderstanding. We have to find what we all have in common and present this in such a way to overcome ignorance and promote understanding."

She also said, "As I look out over this crowd of 'enemies' I hope I am looking at the future commanders of the real war--the war to achieve full human status for both men and women." She concluded with, "Do your part in our common effort to educate, and to liberate not only ourselves but all other men and women." I found her speech to be inspiring and a staggering commentary on our objectives.

When I created the Virginia Prince Award I felt it was time we, as a community, took ourselves seriously. The Awards Banquet was created as an opportunity for us, as a community, to come together as a unified whole and honor those pioneers who made this community possible. It was an opportunity to feel pride in ourselves.

Virginia was to be our first honoree, and she was absolutely the right choice.

The night of the banquet we all assembled in our formal attire. I arranged a reception line featuring our guest of honor Virginia, followed be me, and the rest of the convention staff. That would give everyone an opportunity to meet Virginia personally, and make whatever comments they wanted to the rest of us. Unexpectedly, Lynn Rodriquez from Indiana, approached me and genuflected. It was a complete set-up and a joke. Photos were taken. After that, whenever I got to feeling too high on myself, all I had to do was look at that picture and remind myself, it was a joke.

When it came time to present Virginia with her honor, I was well aware that all previous events, mine included, provided a few personal growth workshops, lots of parties, and lots of fun. Virginia understood this too, so when Naomi stood up and presented Virginia with a pair of gilded falsies, she laughed and took it for the joke it was meant to be. We all had a good laugh, and Virginia went to sit down. Apparently, she thought receiving a pair of false tits for laughs was the end of it. Then I stood up and presented her with the plaque which was named after her, and explained its significance. Virginia was dumbstruck. I had never seen her speechless. The only words she could muster was to promise to be around until all twenty four nameplates on the plaque were filled. Since Virginia was approaching eighty, that was quite a promise to make. All the attendees stood and gave her a standing ovation. Our community gave Virginia Prince a standing ovation. I believed I saw a tear or two. It was an extraordinary way to end the convention.

Before the convention, I founded the Tiffany Club, founded NACD Inc. which enabled me to purchase the Wayland House, founded the Tapestry, created and coordinated a number of events and conferences, created and presented a bunch of acknowledgements and awards, founded IFGE and founded the IFGE Convention. It was beginning to look like and feel like a one person dog and pony show. All my work was being done in a 7'X10' space in my bedroom. The objective was to create a community of people who would work together for mutual benefit, and support each other. I could not create in my bedroom a publication and community that would affect the lives of thousands and in time perhaps millions of people. The stamps and bookkeeping alone would have been mind boggling. I needed to sell the dream, build a local team of people who could get me out of my bedroom and help get the work done, and build a world-wide cadre of leaders, educators and friends who could build a community and build a family.

History part 26

ADDENDUM (Could someone put this text where it belongs?)

To be inserted between the last paragraph on the banquet, and the last paragraph, my plea for help.

There was one last event before the convention concluded, that was the Farewell Brunch. That was when everyone packed up their wardrobes, changed back into their civilian selves, and joined the other participants to say goodbye. The problem was, when the participants changed back into their civilian selves, nobody knew who anybody was. It was like playing a huge game of 'mystery identity I've got a secret.' There were gradual recognitions, then hugs and tears abound, and promises to meet again at the next convention.

A few, such as my co-director Elaine, and our financial coordinator Yvonne, absolutely despised the idea of returning to their previous lives. We discussed the 1988 convention with

Elaine, the hotel's sales manager, who invited us to dine with her in the Portico, the hotel's four-star French restaurant. We were seated next to Trini Lopez and his entourage, and two tables away from Cary Grant's reserved table. For the most part, I had no idea what I was eating. I recognized the snails, and loved the baked lobster tails wrapped in bacon, but most of the rest of it was just yellow, and some of it was wet. Obviously I was no connoisseur of French cooking.

Yvonne finished paying the bills, we discussed plans for the '88 convention, then went our separate ways. I left for some quiet time at Sheila's in Pittsburgh, to relax, discuss the future, and eat some food that I recognized. Sheila and I shared one thing in common, she loved to cook, and I loved to eat.

History part 27

Building a local team would have been difficult, even if the Tiffany Club had not left me. As for publishing the Tapestry, running the convention, building a community and an international network of organizations and support services, and a cadre of leaders and teachers, well, all I could do was the best I could do. IFGE's board of directors held its first session at the '87 convention. To say I was apprehensive would have been an understatement. (1.) I had no one to help me with the work. (2.) The board was bound to see themselves as business managers, or bosses, rather than leaders or educators. (3.) With a few exceptions, the board members were from all over the country, which was bound to make communications difficult. (4.) IFGE was created to provide the community with the tools that would empower the community. (5.) Worst of all, I doubted the board shared my vision. I truly feared the board would switch their focus from building and empowering our community to politics and money. If IFGE became dominated by politics and money, then all my work would have become wasted, and my vision destroyed. If that happened then my reason for being would have been destroyed. It was a scary time for me.

Our first board consisted of the best people I could find. Pat West (Maine) who was chosen to be chairperson. Having Pat as chairperson meant that I didn't have to run the meetings. That was the first good sign that IFGE would not be the 'Merissa Sherrill Lynn show'. It was also good because Pat was relatively local and we could talk, and Pat had been with me since the beginning and I felt confident she understood the long-term objectives. Besides that I really liked her, and I always found it easier to work with a friend.

The board also included Eve Burchert (Illinois), Renee Chevalier (N. New York), Joanna Clark (S. California), Cheryl Costa (W. New York), Holly Cross (Massachusetts), Sheila Kirk (Pennsylvania), Betty Ann Lind (Virginia), Naomi Owen (Illinois), Virginia Prince (S. California), Roger Peo (N. New York), Ellen Summers (Oregon), Helen Tibbetts (New Hampshire), Elaine Willey (Michigan), and me (New Hampshire).

When it came to creating the IFGE board of directors, I made many mistakes. The first mistake was spiritual. I was motivated by the calling of my spirit, and defined success by how much good we did. For most of the people I met, success seemed to be defined by politics and profit. My mistake was I did not surround myself with people of similar spirit, or who shared a similar definition of success.

My next mistake was bringing in good people from all over the country. When we were separated by such distance, being able to get together no more than four times a year, there was no possible way to adequately manage IFGE. The distance alone was bound to lead to chaos.

My Next mistake was not making sure people who accepted a position on the board clearly understood and accepted why IFGE was created in the first place. Without understanding IFGE's purpose and objectives, people were bound to create their own agenda, thereby rendering IFGE irrelevant.

My biggest mistake was making selection to the board a democratic process.

History part 28

The purpose for creating IFGE was to build a community and to provide that community with the tools to enable it to work together for the benefit of all. People always asked me, "What's in it for me?" My answer was always the same, "The opportunity to do something for somebody else."

The great dangers of making the selection of Board members a democratic process was to take the vision of IFGE and put it in the hands of people who for the most part had their own self-interest at heart, did not understand IFGE's vision or purpose, IFGE's objective, or disagreed with the objective.

The purpose of the IFGE board of directors was to create a cadre of leaders who could work together while putting the community to work for the benefit of all. Caring about the members of our community, their families, and the society in which they lives was absolutely necessary. By democratically selecting board members, those members would be chosen on the basis of fame, popularity, external expertise or some other irrelevant quality. By electing dynamic, aggressive and mean spirited business executives, lawyers, and military leaders with their own ways of doing things, instead of electing loving people with vision guaranteed a board with private agendas, who neither understood the vision or purpose of IFGE, or disagreed with its objectives. With board members selected from across the nation, distance would make it difficult to communicate and find opportunities to work together.   It was a disaster waiting to happen.

I saw my role in this enterprise as the Founding Director.   As such it was my responsibility to keep IFGE focused on its objective, to work independently and to pitch in where I could.   If there was such a thing as a flow chart, I would be in a fluffy white cloud in the upper left hand corner of the chart, to be neither above nor below anyone, there to work with everyone, to be the boss of no one, and to be bossed by no one.   Since most of the folks on the board would base their roles on their external expertise and their own private agendas, and the role of Founding Director was not a position found on most flow charts, there was an excellent possibility that neither me personally nor my position would not be respected.   Again, it was a disaster waiting to happen.

All of that aside, the immediate problem facing the '87 IFGE board of directors was to find me the help I needed to make it work.   I needed a compatible team made up of compassionate and insightful people.   The selection of Pat West as chairperson of the board was an excellent start.   During the board meeting, Vernon Porter, a long-time friend of the Tiffany Club, and a dance wear vendor from Waltham Massachusetts, approached the board with a proposal.   Not only did Vernon own a store, he owned the whole building.   Except for a dance studio where Vernon taught square dancing, the second floor of his building was completely unoccupied, which he would be willing to rent to IFGE for minimal cost. In addition to this miracle, Yvonne Cook, the convention financial coordinator, told the board that if they approved of Vernon's offer, Yvonne would move to Waltham to help out. The board approved.   With Yvonne as a working partner, all good things appeared possible.

That summer Yvonne came to Boston for a visit. The purpose was to start getting the offices ready for occupancy, find Yvonne a place to live, and to have some fun. The fun consisted of attending Tiffany's Spring Outing in Provincetown. 1987 was the first I was not the year's coordinator, and I was eager to attend as a pure participant without being responsible for anything. Besides, I wanted to introduce P-town to Yvonne, or vise versa.

Attending the Spring Outing was for me a Mother Hen act. The Outing was one of my babies, and 1987 was the first year I had nothing to do with running it. Admittedly, I was a bit concerned, but Laura, the newly elected Tiffany president, and Joan, the newly elected treasurer, were co-coordinators, and they did a splendid job. They had arranged for the Boatslip Inn, one of the finest motels in P-town. The event was well attended, and the scheduling was superb, from the catered seafood reception, to the afternoon T-dance complete with our own band, the evening banquet, to the catered farewell brunch. The lasting portrait of the event was of Yvonne.

Laura had placed us in room 16, which was up a hidden stairwell, down a dark quiet hall to a lovely and very private room with a private balcony overlooking the motel's large deck. The room had a gorgeous view of P-town harbor and all of Cape Cod Bay, from P-town clear around Cape Cod's shore to Plymouth. Laura couldn't have given us a more pleasant room. The picture was of Yvonne, suspended in space hanging off our balcony. Yvonne was going to be my working partner, IFGE's Director of Operations, the chairperson of IFGE's finance committee, and treasurer of IFGE's national convention. Yvonne was going to be a primary representative of IFGE, representing our community's dig nity and pride not only to ourselves, but to society as a whole. Imagine my pride seeing my working partner and our Director of Operations, and dignified representative of our community hanging off our balcony like an orangutan.

One of the Outing's programs was a Saturday afternoon party featuring Tiffany's own rock 'n roll band, the 'Not Quite Ready for Surgery Band'. The band consisted of Jessie, Carol, Billie and Christie on drums. They were surprisingly good. However, Christie on drums presented problems. An army incident had left her deaf as a post. Christie on drums gave new meaning to the term 'marching to the beat of a different drummer'. None of the other musicians knew what the heck she was doing. It was syncopated rhythm at its best.

Christie marched to a different drummer for many reasons. I met her when I first opened the Wayland House in 1980. She was looking for a place to stay for a short time. She announced that she was transsexual, and since Tiffany Club was mostly cross-dressers, she only needed a place to stay for a couple of weeks until she found a place to live. When I closed the Wayland House down eighteen years later, Christie was still there.

Christie was the original Tiffany Club biker chick. She loved to cruise the countryside on her ancient Harley Davidson motorcycle, which looked like it was right out of a 1950's Marlon Brando movie. Our neighborhood was well populated with dogs. One dog was a gigantic red dog with enormous feet, we called 'Bigfoot'. Bigfoot was still a puppy and wanted to play. He wanted to play with Christie's motorcycle. Nothing happened to Bigfoot, but he nearly totaled both the motorcycle and Christie. To add to her 'biker chick' image, Christie would come to the parties with obscene tattoos drawn on her arms. After all, she did have an image to uphold.

Christie was a good mechanic, and eventually got her bike up and running again. She also liked to build things, and turned her bedroom into a workshop. She was the only woman I ever knew who had a table saw in her bedroom. One of her projects was to build an airplane. The garage was filled with red and white airplane parts, and it was not unusual to drive into the parking lot and see an airplane wing sticking out of Christie's bedroom window. Her airplane actually flew.

She was an extraordinary person to know, and I will never forget her standard response to any question or statement presented to her.   "EH?"

History part 30

After Yvonne went back to Indiana, I was left alone again. Making it until Yvonne moved to Waltham looked a little scary. I was still serving as executive secretary for the Tiffany Club, managing the house, trying to put together the next issue of the Tapestry which had turned into a monster, and prepare for the next Coming Together convention, which was scheduled for the end of February '88. I was still trying to do everything from my room in the basement.

By January 1988 I was still in my room in the basement trying to do everything. I called my room The Cave, because it was cold, dank, unheated except for a small space heater, and filled with cobwebs. In addition to the discomfort of the Cave, there were other problems, such as January '88 was miserable, even by Massachusetts standards. The air was wet and heavy, creating a cold that penetrated the bones. The snow, what little we had of it, came down as slush and was quickly frozen. An unrelenting wind, we called the Montreal Express, drove the wet cold into the Cave.

The convention was pressing down on me, barely five weeks away, and I had to be ready.   I had to compose the final let ter which contained critical logistical information, and send it out to the participants. The final marketing needed to be done, as did the typesetting for registration packages, posters, signs, and workshop handouts. I needed to finish the job descriptions and logistics with my staff, and work out the final conference details with the hotel.

In addition Tapestry Issue #52 was unfinished. I was under pressure to complete the work and have it ready for distribution prior to the convention. I had another 150 to 200 hours of labor before I was ready to send it to the printer. I still had the Mailbag, the Directory of Organizations and the Personal Listings to typeset. My computer equipment, to say nothing of my computer skills, were totally inadequate for the job, so I had to do the artwork and paste-up by hand.

I also had my work for Tiffany to do, and it was time for Tiffany's annual billing. There were nearly 800 notices to send out, and my rinky-dink computer barely had enough RAM to compose a letter. That meant the billing had to be done by hand. A basketful of overdue correspondence had stacked up on my desk.

Pat West had retired as IFGE's chairperson, which left me as acting chair. That meant I had to prepare for the Board of Directors meeting, which included setting the agenda, and preparing the financial report. In the meantime people in crisis were constantly calling at all hours, and their needs took precedence over all else.

There was another problem. I had come down with the flu. My illness coupled with my work load had made me a quivering mess, a condition that was obvious to everyone. My friend Terri, and housemate, tried to cheer me up by bringing me a cartoon of a disheveled convulsing secretary draped over her typewriter, shoes off, stocking sagging around her ankles, whimpering, "God! I love this place." I did love this place, and the cartoon did cheer me up, but I needed a break. For me, taking a break meant putting on something warm and taking a spiritually refreshing walk around my house.

History part 31

By suburban standards, the Wayland House was remote. It sat at the end of a dead end street, overlooking endless conservation land cut by the meandering Sudbury River. The view from our back yard was a panoramic waterscape that stretched for miles, clear to Prescott Hill, a bump on the horizon. The sunsets were breathtaking. One of the big dogs we had as neighbors, was Babu, a gigantic black Newfoundland. She looked more like a bear than a dog. The moment I stepped out the door, there was Babu, happily wagging her big floppy tail, slobbering, waiting for her daily pat.

Babu accompanied me as I walked, for which I was very grateful. I was feeling really lousy, very tired and not very stable. Babu helped hold me up, and she was warm. The lawn and driveway was crusted over with frozen snow that looked like polished marble. The mess in the driveway was the result of me being too cheap to have it plowed, and too tired to shovel. My bridal-wreath bush in the front yard was crushed by ice, its glistening branches entwined like the legs of a thousand spiders. Lining one side of my property was a neat row of pine trees, standing tall and straight like soldiers protecting the property. However the first tree in the row stood scarred and broken, it's decapitated crown was missing and its branches lay broken on the ground. It stood like a sacrificed warrior, protecting the rest of the trees from the ravages of nor 'eastern storms which blew in from the North Atlantic.

Lining the other side of my property was a line of maple trees, standing leafless and naked. Their branches reached out like boney fingers, crackling frozen in the wind. An incandescent dusting of snow, like powdered alabaster, sifted down from the ashen sky, covering everything, including myself, with a fine crystalline frosting. It was magically beautiful, a kind of beauty that needed to be seen and felt with the soul. With Babu by my side, I temporarily forgot my illness and my workload.

Across the wetlands, the rising and falling of the river had created a heaving blanket of broken ice. The spooky sound of breaking ice drifted across the wetlands which disguised memories of a carpet of purple flowers and the sweet songs of red-winged blackbirds. The scene that during the summer which was flush with life and beauty, was now hyperborean, barren and cold, its life smothered beneath the ice. To be surrounded by such hibernal beauty refreshed my spirit and reminded me that I owned a little piece of Nature's cathedral, and I could worship in it every day.

Feeling refreshed, it was time to go back to the Cave, and back to work. My health was no better, my workload was no smaller, and the pressure kept growing. Twelve hour work days turned into twenty four hour work days. A night's sleep turned into short catnaps. My eyes hurt and had turned red and swollen from staring at the computer monitor. My fingers ached from constant pounding on the keyboard. The rapid clack of the daisy-wheel printer had become part of my nervous system. The metal shelving I used as a bookcase was strewn with hundreds of pictures and biographies for the personal listings section, and the deep pile brown carpeting was re-carpeted with paper. The Cave was closing in around me, and I began to suffocate and my flu was getting worse. The stuff I was coughing up had turned green. I tried to ward of the chill I stuffed the cracks around the windows with blankets and foam rubber, wrapped myself in a queen-sized comforter, chewed aspirin like nonpareils, and drank cough syrup and cold medicine like coffee. It didn't work. After except for the irrepressible coughing, and the cool trickles of sweat dripping down my neck.   The stabbing ring of the telephone interrupted my trance-like labors.   It was Niela Miller.

History part 32

Niela was coordinating a presentation to the staff of Emerson Hospital in Concord, just a few miles from my home.   She asked me to be on her panel.   I was too exhausted, too sick and overworked to accept her invitation, so I accepted her invitation.   I was in desperate need of a break and was too tired to sleep.   Giving a lecture for a few hours sounded like a great, albeit stupid, idea.

After a refreshing steamy hot shower I donned my best professional business drag, a grey wool pantsuit and full length London Fog trench coat, I was out the door.   My car wouldn't start.   Finally, after a half hour it started, but it was stuck in the snow.   As I tried to push it out of the frozen slush, I heard the sound of popping stitches in the crotch of my pants.   Expending more energy than I had, I freed the car and drove off, weaving like a drunk.

On my way to the hospital I passed Walden Pond, Thoreau's hideaway. The peaceful harmony of the Pond was a beautiful and historic symbol for those of us who loved the natural world.   Thoreau was right.   As I passed the Pond I was overwhelmed by a coughing fit.   The blast of a car horn alerted me that I had driven into the wrong lane.   The image of the black car bearing down on me and the open-mouthed terrified expression of its driver, was imprinted like the outline of a flashbulb on my retinas.   Blinded and gagging, I swerved to avoid killing somebody, namely myself, and collided with a frozen bank of snow.   A little more alert, but still nauseous and occasionally succumbing to a coughing fit, I made it to the hospital without further incident

When I stepped out of my car I noticed a particularly cool draft on my crotch, but paid it little mind. Jenny, the other member of Niela's panel, parked beside me. Looking as elegant as usual, she greeted me. We exchanged nods, and she said, "Hello Merissa. It's good to see you my dear. My goodness you look awful!" I congratulated her on her perspicacity, and assured her I felt as bad as I looked.

We walked, well, Jenny walked, I staggered, to the hospital. Niela met us in the lobby. After commenting on how sick I looked, Niela escorted us toward the lecture hall. Frankly I was getting sick of people telling me how sick I looked. When we passed a mirror I noticed I had a little white tail. When I reached back to explore, I found the crotch of my pants was completely ripped out and my camisole was hanging out.

When we entered the lecture hall, in addition to being completely bare-assed with my underwear hanging out, I was feeling totally awful, with sweat pouring off me as if I had just stepped out of a shower, and I smelled like the floor of Marci's sheep barn. I walked sideways into the room trying to conceal my exposed crotch, and stay away from anyone with good olfactories. Seventy-five medical professionals studied my every move. It occurred to me the table we were to sit at might not have been draped, which would have made my problem obvious to everyone which would have humiliated me beyond description. Such a view would not have helped my credibility as a speaker. The table was skirted, thank God. Despite my being sicker than the proverbial dog, my constant coughing and bare ass, the lecture concluded without further incident.

All things considered, the lecture went well. When we were done a dozen or so people thanked me for coming, and a few recommended I go see a doctor. I gathered myself together quickly, excused myself and left the room, leaving Jenny and

Niela to deal with the questions and answers. Although I could barely see, hurt from stem to stern, was wobbly and disoriented, I drove home without further incident.

When I returned home my clothes went into a garbage bag, and my body went into a nice hot bath where I stayed until I pruned. Then it was back to work. When I sat down to work, nothing had changed. I was anesthetized, my brain benumbed, the only sound was the incessant click of computer keys being pressed. After another two days, my hands turned arthritic, I couldn't see, and all around me became a fata morgana, images without substance. I tried to stand, and collapsed in a heap on the floor.

For the next three weeks I remembered nothing, not eating, not going to the bathroom, not leaving my bed. My phone went unanswered, and my tasks uncompleted. The stuff I coughed up had turned a dark green. Robin E, a member of the IFGE Board, and my friend, checked up on me. She loaded me into her car, and took me to the emergency room of Emerson Hospital. I had lost twenty five pounds, suffered exhaustion, and my flu had turned into pneumonia. The doctor made it clear that I was lucky to still be alive.

The doctor looked familiar; a handsome young man with Lebanese features, short dark hair, balding, wearing wire-rimmed glasses. He was at Niela's lecture, and took pleasure in reminding me he was one of the folks who had suggested I see a doctor. He wanted to check me in, but I refused. No money, no time, too much to do. He grumbled, loaded me up with codeine cough syrup, which tasted exactly like the stuff I got in the army, and erythromycin, then he sent me on my way.

Having lost three weeks, and with the Convention just two weeks away, it was clear none of the projects that needed to be done prior to the convention was going to be completed.

In my attempt to accomplish everything, I had accomplished nothing, and I had nearly killed myself.

History part 33

I began 1988 by failing to accomplish anything, by succumbing to pneumonia and exhaustion, and by experiencing the third most embarrassing moment of my life. What a splendid way to start the year. I had to ask myself what else could go wrong. The answer was simple. I was still sick, I still hadn't finished what I needed to finish, and I had to drive out to Chicago by myself in a Dodge POS made of plastic and tin that had the durability and dependability of a wet cardboard box, and I had a convention to run. I had driven to Chicago at least twice a year since 1983 and knew the route by heart, but this time I was alone and a mental and physical wreck. Also, it was the middle of winter and I had to drive through the Berkshires, the Catskills, the Shwangunks, the Poconos, the Alleghenies, and across the northern Midwest on slick roads loaded with eighteen-wheeler trucks and police cars. It was going to be cold, icy, scary and dangerous as hell.

When it came to leave I loaded the car with an air mattress, a generous supply of blankets and pillows, cough syrup and medicine. Every cranny of remaining space was packed with suitcases, garment bags, convention material, books, posters, administrative supplies, recording equipment and music. Even if there were someone to travel with me, the only space available was on the roof.

Out on the highway the car handled like a cod fish, weaving and wobbling all over the place, scraping the pavement every time I hit a bump or crack in the road. The best I could manage was 50 mph. At that rate it would take forever to travel the 1100 miles to Chicago. Personally, I loved long drives by myself. It was healing, meditative and quiet.

Beautiful landscapes and sky drifted by, without obscene or hysterical phone calls, and peer pressure, usually self-inflicted, to get things done. The only mental exercise was enjoying the scenery, watching for wildlife, listening to classical music and counting out-of-state once removed license plates.

My first stop was Port Jervis, Pennsylvania. Port Jervis was a misnomer. The only water in the area was the Delaware River, which at that point was barely deep enough to float a rubber ducky, and the only Port was Manischewicz. I wrapped myself warm and cozy in my blankets and pillows and dozed off. When I awoke, it was the proverbial dark and dreary night, and very cold. When I got back on the highway the road had turned to black ice. That slowed me down to a crawl. At that pace it would have taken me longer than forever to get to Chicago. When I creeped past the town of Lord's Valley it felt like I was making progress, but then I got trapped behind an orange Schneider tandem truck whose rear was fishtailing worse than I was, and boxed in by a huge yellow JB Hunt truck which was who was in as much trouble as I was. I was trapped, and stayed trapped until I reached Scranton. What was once a lovely one hour drive through the Pennsylvania countryside from Port Jervis to Scranton turned into a six hour journey of pure terror.

The lights of trucks finally left me before I turned for Scranton. I was not sorry to see them go, but their departure did not help. The driving got worse. An opaque fog settled in. It was like trying to drive inside a glass of milk. Scranton was a large town, but it was invisible behind the cloudy veil. The night Montage Ski area were usually a landmark beacon, but they were gone. The only light was the refracted glow of my own headlights. Out in the gloom there were bound to be more trucks, or other idiot drivers like me, or even breakdowns on the side of the road, one of which could have been me at any moment. The road was still a sheet of black ice and I was a hockey puck sliding all over the place. The city didn't exist. The mountains didn't exist. What as in front of me and behind me didn't exist. The hills had become obstacles, tall and steep, and I couldn't see a damned thing. The only way I could make any progress at all was to drive in the gravel on the soft shoulder, and pray there was nothing in the way.

The knowledge that Interstate 81, especially around Scranton, and Interstate 80 were always under construction conjured images of bulldozers, concrete barriers and deep holes as I inched along keeping a bleary eye out for anything or anyone else doing the same thing. I was in the Twilight Zone. To say it was spooky scary would have been an unfathomable understatement.

History part 34

When I reached the crest of the hill two phosphorescent blazing red eyes stared at me through the fog. My first thought was, "My God, the Demon Spawn from the Amityville Horror was real!" They were road flares, surrounded by a collection of reflective triangle street hazard warnings. Then a prodigious collection of flashing lights; white lights, red lights, blue lights, and a plethora of vehicles; cop cars, crashed cars, ambulances, emergency vehicles, fire trucks and tow trucks came into view, as did a lot of nutsy crazy people staggering about hugging each other, hysterically waving their arms and wringing their hands. My second thought was, "My God, I'm in the middle of a California style multi car crash!" Then I saw the bus. A large Greyhound bus had spun around on the ice, flipped over the guard rail backwards and had started to roll down the mountain. A policeman waving a long red flashlight like a light saber, tried to guide me safely around the accident. Being guided safely around a bad accident while driving downhill on black ice was not an easy thing to do, especially while pirouetting down the road, quietly screaming. I never did find out how many people were hurt, or worse.

Unnerved by the accident and wide awake for the first time since I left Wayland, I creeped warily along. After what seemed like an eternity I reached Interstate 80, the main highway across Pennsylvania to Chicago. The fog had lifted, the ice was gone and the highway returned to being almost normal. I pulled into the first rest stop I came to, the Buckhorn Truck Plaza. In my rickety little car surrounded by trucks, it felt like being Orpheus in the Underworld. I parked behind an orange Schneider tandem truck and for a second wondered if it was the same truck I was stuck behind earlier. Then I pulled out the pillows and blankets, made myself warm and cozy, and passed out.

When I woke up the Schneider truck had been replaced by a white Guaranteed Overnight Delivery (GOD) truck with its initials boldly emblazoned on its rear. When I woke up the word 'GOD' was imprinted across my windshield. It occurred to me that I had been on the road for nearly twenty four hours and I was barely a quarter of the way to Chicago which was normally an eighteen hour trip. This road trip was a damnation, and 'GOD' could very well have had a hand in it.

As was expected, when I got back on I-80, it was under construction. There were the usual concrete barriers, bulldozers, backhoes, dump trucks, and signs saying "Under Construction" which elicited a 'No Shit' from me. There were also the flashing signs saying "Speed limit 45 MPH." Since that was about as fast as I could go anyway, that didn't pose a problem. However it did cause a problem for truckers in a hurry, and for construction vehicles and eighteen-wheelers too wide for the one lane traffic.   It also caused a problem for the numerous deer trying to cross the road The saddest aspect of traveling across Pennsylvania was the large number of deer that became roadkill.   Western Pennsylvania is an especially lovely part of the country with its mountains, rivers, national and state forests and wildlife.   It was my favorite part of my trips to Chicago.   I was just east of Du Bois when I found myself trapped behind a green Mayflower Van Lines eighteen-wheeler. A small herd of deer gathered by the highway. Suddenly a beautiful doe, fat and healthy, dashed onto the highway in front of the truck.   The truck driver tried, but couldn't avoid hitting the deer, and it exploded off the truck's bumper and disappeared beneath the truck.   I was stuck, I couldn't weave or stop, and couldn't avoid hitting the deer myself. After I thumped over the deer's remains and skidded on its whatever, I pulled off to the side of the highway and threw up.

History part 35

The rest of my journey across Pennsylvania was relatively without incident.   However the sides of the highway were still littered with the carcasses of dead deer.   Each deer I saw reminded me of the deer I hit, and left me with the heartsick feeling that I was in some way responsible for turning so many of Nature's beautiful creatures into food for crows. Seeing so much death on the highway made me feel a great injustice had been done, the kind of cruel injustice that happened every time an innocent creature with the same right to live as me, came into contact with people and their machines. I couldn't wait to get out of Pennsylvania and put the carnage behind me.

Exit 13 in Brookville was a landmark.   It was the exit I used going to or coming from Sheila's house in Pittsburgh.   It marked the end of the Alleghenies.   It marked the end of the highway carnage and a return to relatively safe driving. Structures such as the Exxon station, the little brown restaurant and a Days Inn were like old friends, or at least salient milestones. It was also the halfway point to Chicago. As much as I enjoyed Pennsylvania's beauty I preferred staying alive. Exit 13 meant I was barely an hour from the Ohio border and relative safety, which made exit 13 a very welcome exit.

Passing under the Ohio Highway Commission's big blue arch welcoming travelers to Ohio, gave me both a sense of relief and a nervous sense of trepidation. I had traveled back and forth across Ohio many times. It was a long trip, with fine roads and a lot of police. I had never made it across Ohio without being stopped for speeding, faulty equipment, a breakdown or something. I was once stopped for wearing earphones. I was also stopped because the officer thought I was carrying too many passengers. This time since I was still sick and exhausted, and the car was wobbling about like a doodlebug on too much caffeine, I fully expected to be stopped because some officer thought I was drunk, or for driving erratically, or because they thought my rearview mirror was obscured, or because he just felt like it. Travelling across Ohio was a paranoid person's nightmare. Ohio was really out to get me. Passing under the blue arch felt like entering the web of a trapdoor spider, or a black hole where I threw away my peace-of-mind never to see it again.

My journey began with a refreshing nap, and gathering a good supply of road food, which usually consisted of an ample supply of MacDonald's cheeseburgers and fries, a half-pound of sliced Genoa salami, a large bag of Wise potato chips or Smart Food popcorn, and several bottles of Poland Spring water. I doubt Julia Childs would have approved of my culinary choices, but it did keep my mouth busy and me going. I began my trip across Ohio warily looking for the police. My absolute surprise I made all the way across Ohio without hassle. Indiana was one of my favorite states. The toll booth tender was always friendly, and the land had a horizontal symmetry, it was as flat as a flounder, but very green and gorgeous. It also contained two of my favorite landmarks. Before I began working for the Transgender community, I made my living by teaching skiing, which meant I was used to living in the hills. The first landmark was the Mount Ashmont Skiway. The trees at the bottom of the hill were taller than the hill itself. That Mount Ashmont had a functioning chairlift was mind boggling. When I was a kid I lived on a glacial esker, a small hill of gravel. My backyard had enough of a slope for me to learn how to make a snow-plow turn. My backyard was bigger than Mount Ashmont. Where the hell were Indiana skiers supposed to ski? I doubted Indiana would ever become known as the hub of the alpine universe.

My other favorite landmark was in the city of Gary. Gary was a rusty old steel city. The rotting old foundries stood like wrecked warships stranded on the beach. On the out-skirts of town there as a large field of slag, as flat as Indiana itself. In the middle of the slag heap was a small sooty pond or a large puddle in which someone had the effrontery to build a tiny island, plant a tree of unknown genus, and place a picnic table beneath it. It was the saddest excuse for a park I had ever seen, but I loved it. It had character. It made me want to grab a bag of potato chips, a flask of water, a couple of cheeseburgers and go have a picnic. Where else could you have lunch on a slag heap

From Gary it was a short trip over an atrophied decrepit old bridge into Chicago. My trip felt like it was practically at an end. I had the misfortune of entering Chicago during rush hour. Cars filled with irate drivers sharing obscene hand signals, were stacked bumper to bumper as far as I could see. Besides being excruciatingly slow, my poor fevered body felt the da-dump da-dump of every crack and pothole in the road

Each horn blat was like a bee sting to my ears. It took melonger cross Chicago to my hotel as it did to drive across Indiana. It normally took me eighteen hours to drive to Chicago. This time it took me three days, but I made it.

History part 36

I arrived at the Ramada in my usual manner, looking and feeling like hell, totally exhausted and covered in junk food crumbs. I looked like a walking bird feeder. A handsome affable young man, smartly dressed in his burgundy and black uniform, pulling a bellhop's cart behind him, greeted me. "Welcome back Ma'am. Nice to see you again." Given my aesthetically tragic appearance, fulsome physical state of being and state of mind, his sunny greeting was like taking a barrel of sour pickles (me) and dropping it into a field of daisies.

After attending to precursory duties such as hotel registration, announcing my presence with a token stroll through the bar, dumping my convention stuff in a heap in our registration room, dumping my luggage in a heap on my bed, amply rewarding the bellhop for his delightful greeting and hard work, I passed out. I slept like a rock for 24 hours, and was awoken by the annoying ping - ping - ping of the telephone. It was Yvonne demanding my immediate attention. Yvonne was once again serving as Convention Registrar, Vendor and Financial Coordinator, and was a newly elected member of our Board. She was right, it was time for me to get cleaned up and back to work.

My first choice of ensemble was a tan cambric dress. It was just professional enough to look professional, casual enough to be comfortable, and attractive enough to be unobtrusive or unpretentious. There were problems. Due to my illness I had lost considerable weight, and none of my clothes fit. I had been undergoing hormone therapy for a decade, and had developed a fair cleavage, of which I was immeasurably-proud. The dress had a deep plunging neckline, and my boobs were hanging out.   I was very proud that I had boobs large enough to hang out of anything, but modest enough to think walking around the hotel with my boobs hanging out was probably not a good idea.   Fortunately, I had safety pins - problem solved.   There was another problem.   As providence would have it, we landed in another record breaking heat wave, and I hated heat.   Fortunately my cambric dress was relatively cool. When I reached the registration room Yvonne was hard at work.   She was wearing a red and white striped T-shirt and dungaree shorts.   We were in Chicago, one of the coldest cities in America, in the middle of the winter, and Yvonne, who had the metabolism of a gecko and hated any temperature under 85, was wearing a T-shirt and shorts.   It was a world gone mad.

The moment I stepped into the registration room it was like diving into a pool filled with piranhas.   It seemed everybody wanted a piece of me.   There was no peace and no escape. Yvonne did a superb job coordinating the vendors and volunteers, and keeping me from getting eaten alive.   Bette Lee Johnson, the convention coordinator, also did a superb job, and was able to take the load almost completely off my shoulders.   Bette was doing such a fine job she left me with nothing more to do than run the morning staff meetings, monitor committee meetings and workshop sessions, drink gallons of coffee while engaging in endless brainstorming sessions, political –outreach -educational activities with

strangers on behalf of IFGE and our community, walk the corridors and sit at head tables, looking important.
While talking to Yvonne it occurred to me that other than a few dry cheeseburgers and a bag of popcorn, I hadn't eaten in over three days.   So, I grabbed Yvonne by the arm and hauled her off to the Copper Trellis for lunch.   We found a

nice private table behind a profusion of plastic jungle vegetation.   I told her all about my sad tale of my winter woes and my memorable drive from Wayland to Chicago.   With a catatonic look, spooning her soup and picking plastic leaves off the table, she waited until I finished feeling sorry for myself. Then we got down to business.

History part 37

Building a local team would have been difficult, even if the Tiffany Club had not left me.   As for publishing the Tapestry, running the convention, building a community and an international network of organizations and support services, and a cadre of leaders and teachers, well, all I could do was the best I could do.   IFGE's board of directors held its first session at the '87 convention.   To say I was apprehensive would have been an understatement.   (1.) I had no one to help me with the work.   (2.) The board was bound to see themselves as business managers, or bosses, rather than leaders or educators.   (3.) With a few exceptions, the board members were from all over the country, which was bound to make communications difficult.   (4.) IFGE was created to provide the community with the tools that would empower the community.   (5.) Worst of all, I doubted the board shared my vision.   I truly feared the board would switch their focus from building and empowering our community to politics and money.

If IFGE became dominated by politics and money, then all my work would have become wasted, and my vision destroyed.
If that happened then my reason for being would have been destroyed.   It was a scary time for me.

Our first board consisted of the best people I could find.   Pat West (Maine) who was chosen to be chairperson.   Having Pat as chairperson meant that I didn't have to run the meetings that was the first good sign that IFGE would not be the

'Merissa Sherrill Lynn show'. It was also good because Pat was relatively local and we could talk, and Pat had been with me since the beginning and I felt confident she understood the long-term objectives. Besides that I really liked her, and I always found it easier to work with a friend.

The board also included Eve Burchert (Illinois), Renee Chevalier (N. New York), Joanna Clark (S. California), Cheryl Costa (W. New York), Holly Cross (Massachusetts), Sheila Kirk (Pennsylvania), Betty Ann Lind (Virginia), Naomi Owen (Illinois), Virginia Prince (S. California), Roger Peo (N. New York), Ellen Summers (Oregon), Helen Tibbetts (New Hampshire), Elaine Willey (Michigan), and me (New Hampshire).

When it came to creating the IFGE board of directors, I made many mistakes. The first mistake was spiritual. I was motivated by the calling of my spirit, and defined success by how much good we did. For most of the people I met, success seemed to be defined by politics and profit. My mistake was I did not surround myself with people of similar spirit, or who shared a similar definition of success.

My next mistake was bringing in good people from all over the country. When we were separated by such distance, being able to get together no more than four times a year, there was no possible way to adequately manage IFGE. The distance alone was bound to lead to chaos.

My Next mistake was not making sure people who accepted a position on the board clearly understood and accepted why IFGE was created in the first place. Without understanding

IFGE's purpose and objectives, people were bound to create their own agenda, thereby rendering IFGE irrelevant.

My biggest mistake was making selection to the board a democratic process

History part 38

With things going so well with the convention there wasn't a lot for me to do, so I retired to my room and did what came naturally.   I made a hell of a mess.   I sat in my room like an ascetic monk, strumming a few tunes and contemplating the future of our community while watching jets take-off and land at O'Hare Airport.   I spread out my papers which covered the floor, the furniture and my bed, then threw clothing over any exposed piece of furniture.   It looked like my bedroom back home. It was a habit that did not make me popular with the hotel housekeepers.   Things going smoothly didn't feel natural, and neither did being neat.   Fortunately for my own sense of propriety, I made a nice comfortable mess, and I did have two tiny problems with the awards committee.

At the '87 convention I introduced the VP award so our community could remember its history and honor its pioneers.   At the '88 convention I introduced the Trinity award, a pewter statuette mounted on walnut modeled after IFGE's hands and rose logo. I thought it was beautiful, and spiritually meaningful.   The purpose of the award was to give our community an opportunity to honor its heroes.   My problem was IFGE's awards committee selected me to receive both awards.   I did not create these awards to honor myself.   I created them so our community could reward itself.   For me to receive these awards it was, well, embarrassing.

My objection to receiving the VP award was - it wasn't my turn. There were others who should have had consideration before me.   For instance there was Ariadne Kane, founder of Outreach and Fantasia Fair, the cradle for so many of our community's leaders, including me.   Also there were Sister Mary Elizabeth, Lee Brewster, Carol Beecroft, and many others.   My favorite candidate was the Widow Norton, a San Francisco drag queen who founded the Imperial Court, a fund raising program with chapter's world-wide.   Thanks to the Widow Norton thousands and thousands of dollars had been raised for charities, primarily AIDS research.   She was a true pioneer.   Despite my objections, Ellen Summers, chair of the awards committee, turned to me and said, "My dear, you don't have a damn thing to say about it."

My objections to receiving the Trinity was - I wasn't a hero, and it was a wasted opportunity to find our real heroes. When I created the award I was thinking of folks like Sylvia Rivera from NYC.   She was a street queen who helped instigate the Stonewall riots which led to changing the homophobic per-secution laws in NYC.   She also used her own resources to create 'Bridge over Troubled Waters', a project designed to help keep our kids off the streets.   One of our local gals founded and managed a food bank, serving many people. One of our local female-to male brothers became a minister and made significant inroads into the religious community. Another one of our sisters in Colorado pulled a man from a burning wreck and saved his life.   A sister in Turkey, a Mus-lim nation, took on the Turkish government.   These were heroes.   God only knew how many of our heroic sisters, brothers and friends there were all over the world.   I in-vented the Trinity award to find folks like these and enable our community to acknowledge their contributions and hon-or them.   I did not want the awards to focus attention on me. It was personally awkward, and it trivialized the awards.

History part 39

If my concerns over trivializing the awards, missing an op-portunity to strengthen our community and making me look like a total ass were my only troubles, we were having a suc-cessful convention.   The morning after my lunch with

Yvonne, I returned to the Copper Trellis to indulge in their lovely breakfast buffet. Unfortunately my plebian sense of taste mandated I load up my plate with sausage and eggs, and a banana to offset the cholesterol. As I tried to balance my unbalanced meal while looking for a place to sit, I spotted Sister Mary Elizabeth in her unmistakable navy blue habit.

Sister Mary and I had been friends for many years, and was one of my candidates to receive the VP Award. I first learned of Sister Mary in the mid-70's when she was still known as Joanna Clark. At a time when I was first trying to get my own life in order, I read about a lady in Southern California who was a Navy Seal, left the service to transition, then joined the Army as a WAC to finish her tour of duty. The Army tried to remove her, but she sued them, and won. WOW! I was in the Army once, and I knew that if they had found out I was transsexual they would have thrown me out, and I knew I would never have had the courage to fight them to save my job. I could not imagine me ever being that brave. From then on Joanna was a hero to me.

When she retired, she founded the Renaissance Gender Identity Service in Southern California. In the mid-70's support groups and services, including my own, were like popcorn in a skillet popping up everywhere. Among these services was one created by a female-to-male brother, called the Erickson Educational Foundation. The Erickson Foundation became the Janus Information Foundation which was then absorbed by Joanna's Renaissance Gender Identity Service. Joanna then teamed with a brother, Jude Patton, and Renaissance evolved into the J2CP Gender Information Services.

Joanna gained additional notoriety when during a ceremony on a beach just a stone's throw from ex-President Nixon's compound in San Clemente, Joanna was ordained, and became known as Sister Mary Elizabeth. It was this act, more than any other that connected me to Sister Mary. I was not a religious person, but I was a spiritual person. My excursion into the wilderness provided me with a spiritual awakening, a sense of purpose, and a commitment to use these gifts in a good way. By taking her vows, she answered the calling of her heart and committed herself to a life of doing good. Sister Mary and I came from different places, but arrived in the same place, using the gifts of our souls to dedicate our lives to doing good. We were truly sisters of the soul.

Comportment be damned! When I saw her I put my food down, happily skipped across the floor waving my arms, squealing like a ten year old girl returning to summer camp. After a big warm vigorous hug, Sister Mary introduced me to her companion. Her companion was a plumpish middle-aged woman, wearing a bright red blouse. It was Christine Jorgensen. I lost all sense of orthodox propriety.

I remembered in 1953, when I was a very confused eleven year old, reading the headline 'Ex-GI Becomes Blonde Beauty' splashed across page one of the New York Daily News The headline was complete with an elegant portrait of Christine. She was branded on my memory, a permanent symbol of what was possible. Christine was a celebrity, with movies made and books written of her life. Through her celebrity she had reached thousands, if not millions, of gender conflicted people such as myself. She was known around the world, had been introduced to royalty, and counted some of the most famous Hollywood personalities among her friends. When I finished stammering, fawning and tripping over my own tongue, I invited them to join me for breakfast. There I was, sharing pancakes and coffee and laughter with Christine Jorgensen, chatting with her as if she was regular folks.

History part 40

One of my greatest joys, if not my greatest joy, was to sit with intelligent people, over coffee and food, and share thoughts and ideas. Sitting with Sister Mary and Christine was a delight. It didn't start out that way. It started out uncomfortable, then sad, then delightful. I was a non-smoker. Christine was a chain smoker. She then told me she was terminally ill, but not from the smoking. If I wanted her company I would have to deal with her smoking, so I compromised. I shut up.

The conversation was so pleasant I forgot about her smoking...almost. It was like hiking a gnarly mountain trail while singing a happy mountain song. The rough trail was easy to overlook...almost. She was visibly ill, but in spite of her illness she was in remarkably good spirits, and seemed to be genuinely glad to be with us. She laughed easily, had a warm smile, and kind words for everyone. She was fun to be with, had a rich and loving soul, and sincerely cared about others and the future of the transgender community. I genuinely liked her, and felt truly sad that we were about to lose her. I wondered if, when my time came, I would have anywhere near as much dignity as she did.

Talking with Christine ignited ancient memories. In 1948 I purchased a Science Fiction comic book which featured a story about Doctor Davis and his wife. They had joined an expedition to Mars to populate and settle the planet. The vehicle crashed and everyone but Dr. Davis died. Since his mission was to populate Mars, he turned himself into a woman and impregnated himself. In a twist of irony his wife somehow had survived the crash, and showed up long after Dr. Davis was already a woman and pregnant. I suppose in 1948 this story was supposed to be shocking, but to me it enflamed a longing in my heart that stayed with me my entire life.

In 1952 I came across a copy of 'Life' magazine featuring Christine.   There was a picture of her dressed elegantly in a green satin evening dress.   Perhaps in 1952 Christine was a disturbing phenomenon, but to me she illuminated that deepest dreams could still come true.

Also in 1952 I acquired a copy if 'Mad' magazine which also lampooned Christine.   It implied Christine changed her sex so she could pick up sailors and use the women's restroom. It awakened the awareness that even if used in humor, social attitudes could be intensely cruel.   It didn't matter.

I remembered scouring the storage bags in the attic for bits and pieces of forgotten women's clothing, and searching the trash for discarded clothing.   I took my treasures to a tree house I had built deep in the woods where no one would find them. I also remembered when I joined the army and was stationed in Germany.   I fell in love with a German girl, but was so gender conflicted and so afraid of rejection that I pushed her out of my life before, because eventually my gender conflict was bound to emerge which would force her to reject me, I pushed her out of my life.   For the remainder of my life losing her was the single greatest regret of my life. That made me very afraid and very lonely which in turn led me to numerous suicide attempts and defined the course of the rest of my life.

It also dictated the reason for the course of my education, and to the awareness that there must have been thousands, millions, of people just like me desperate for knowledge and support.   The desire to do good led to the creation of all my projects, including IFGE and the convention.

Since my intention was to help people, and I was in charge of the convention, I needed to get back to work.   As delightful as my visit with Sister Mary and Christine was, I excused myself and went back to work.

For me the workday consisted of coordinating an early morning staff meeting to make sure we were prepared for the day, attending committee meetings, occasionally sharing coffee with someone to discuss ideas for the future of our community, looking in on various sessions to assure myself all was well, sitting at the head table at lunch, looking important, while getting silly with whoever I was sitting next to. With Betty coordinating the convention, Yvonne handling financial matters and

Robin coordinating programs, and everything running as beautifully as it was, there wasn't much for me to do. For me that all changed the night of our awards banquet.

<u>Special Additions</u>

The Lady Slippers

Lady Slipper's part 1

All of my life I had struggled with an intense desire to be a woman. I spent most of my life trying to hide that fact. When I started college I spent eight year trying to understand it, by learning everything I could about psychology, sociology, basically everything trying to why I was the way I was. And, studying philosophy trying to understand such concepts as 'meaning', 'purpose', 'Nature', 'spirit', 'God', and other such metaphysical trivia. All to no avail. I had no idea why I was the way I was, found no meaning in anything, and had no understanding whatever of the nature of my own spirit, much less the nature of God. Up until my encounter with the lady slipper, my life was pretty much pointless.

What the lady slipper taught me was that understanding why I was the way I was, was not important. What was important was that I accept the fact that I was the way I was. It also taught me was because I was the way I was, I had a special gift, not a curse, and that I could use that gift in a good way, to help other people. A little woodland flower gave my life meaning. This revelation was the single most important experience of my life.

I had a gift, and I could use this gift to help people. How? I didn't even know what to call it; much less know where to start. I had heard of the word 'transvestism', but didn't give a damn about clothing, so I knew that wasn't it. It was, however, a good place to start. Since I lived in the White Mountains of New Hampshire, the only place I could go was to the Plymouth State Collage library. It was absolutely devoid of information, so was everyone who worked there. The best they could do was recommend I go to UNH's library. I had already spent eight years in that library to no avail, but I would try again. Sure enough, they still didn't have anything. They did however direct me to SAGA, the Seacoast Area Gay Alliance. Since I wasn't gay, I had no idea what they could to for me.

My issue was I wanted to be a woman. It wasn't about wearing women's clothes, sex, relationships, or any of that trivial stuff. SAGA was about sex and relationship, so sure enough, they couldn't do a thing. They did however, direct me to Peter's Palace Peter's Palace was a XXX bookstore, a tiny boarded up hole in a brick wall in Portsmouth, New Hampshire. I managed to find it, and felt weird going in. I had never been in an adult bookstore before. They had a little pornography, a few magazines and video tapes of people screwing, getting chained and whipped, and getting blow jobs, but nothing on transvestism. I did, however, find a really trashy newspaper called 'FI (female impersonator) News', and a relatively decent magazine called 'Drag'. FI News was mostly sex, and people looking for sex. That held no interest for me. Drag on the other hand was fairly well done, certainly the best I had seen, with a nicely drawn portrait on the cover by someone named Vicky West. Drag was published by Lee Brewster's Mardi Gras, a book store and boutique in New York City catering mostly to people in the female impersonation arts. It was the closest I had come to something useful, but before I ventured to New York I still had a few local options to look into.

I went to talk to Paul, my Bridge partner, who also happened to be a biology professor at UNH. He had a human sexuality course which was the most popular course on campus. If anybody knew anything, he would. I talked to him and he just stared at me as if I had just eaten a centipede. I knew more than he did.

I went home for a visit where I met Sherry. My parents owned a trailer park, and Sherry was a tenant. I was working topless, violently tearing down some old cabins. It's surprising how satisfying a little violence can be. She was tall, lissome, beautiful, a professional model. She came over to me and asked if I thought she was attractive. It was a great come-on, one of the best I ever experienced, and answered 'hell yes.' Next thing I knew I was in her bedroom. She laid out a peignoir, then another, then another. She could see I was interested, so I explained my situation. She responded, "You are who you are, and that's OK!" She was the first person to ever tell me being who I was, was OK. A few short months before I was ready to die for fear of other people, and now someone was telling me it's OK. There's just no way of explaining the power that statement had for me. Thus began a lovely relationship that lasted for years.

In the years we were together we had many wonderful experiences, but the most extraordinary happened in my apartment in the mountains. In the winter I taught skiing for a living. In the summer I took whatever job I could find. That summer Sherry came for a visit. We lay naked on my bed. She fit my body so perfectly there was no way I could separate my body from hers.   She was like a focus for meditation, a magical reality. Without being aware of what happened, I was outside my body watching. It was like what they say happens when you die, and for a while, I wondered. I wandered about the apartment, and noticed the light in the kitchen was still on. Next I wandered into the second bedroom and found a pair of white Winslow tennis shorts, size 34. I went back into my bedroom and kept watching, when I noticed my landlord pull into the driveway in his red Thunderbird. I woke up, put on some clothes and wandered about. Everything I saw was true. The light was on, the shorts were there, and so was my landlord. This experience awoke some old metaphysical questions, if out-of-body experiences were possible, what else was possible? What other dimensions existed? It sure got me to thinking, and it got me to loving Sherry more than I thought was possible.

Lady Slippers Part 2

I loved Sherry, and I wanted her to be happy. I had been in love before, but my gender identity situation motivated me to push them out of my life. As a child of the 1950's and 1960's, I lived in an unusually intolerant age, so my defense was to push people out of my life, to reject them before they rejected me. My problem with Sherry was I had never been happy, and had no idea how to make her happy. We experimented. It seemed that role reversal, to let her be the boss, seemed to work. I was freed from having to decide what would make her happy. It was her responsibility to tell me what would make her happy. Also, I had never been very sexually active. I just wasn't very sexually oriented, which is why I never connected to sexual issues. In my dreams I could respond sexually if I was female. The same was true when I was awake, and since I had no interest in men, this situation caused some problems in real life. With Sherry that wasn't a problem and we experimented in that arena as well. We found obedience and a little discomfort and restraint worked very well. When the sexual juices finally got going, WOW! We couldn't get enough. In time we found a lot of names for our relationship, D&S, which was Dominance-Submission, M&S, which was Master-Slave, B&D, which meant Bondage and Discipline, S&M, which was sado-Masochism

In our searches we found clubs and bars that catered to people with interests similar to ours. Clubs like the 'Club of O', 'Plato's Retreat', 'the Vault', 'Paddles', 'The Mineshaft' and 'Eulenspiegel', which according to my German dictionary meant Owls Mirror. I had no idea what that meant. I originally thought it meant 'forbidden play', but it could have been anything. All I knew was in every XXX store we visited had a section dedicated to B&D and S&M. Obviously we weren't alone. We didn't visit many of these clubs, but we did scour an area in Boston called 'The Combat Zone', an area set aside for the XXX rated trade, bookstores, movies, bars and such. There were a number of topless bars, and Drag bars with names like Over Harry's, Hotel Avery, The Other Side, and most notorious was Jacque's. Jacque's was the place for Drag prostitutes, and dirty Drag shows.

Inside Jacque's was filthy. The air smelled like burned tar, and the floor was sticky from spilled beer, and other things I choose not to think about. The entertainment was Sylvia Sidney, a porky foul smelling drag queen, who wore a cold cream jar filled with dog shit for a ring. Outside the bar looked like the corner ice cream parlor with a nice clean sidewalk and street, and white and green striped awnings over the windows. It was sleaze taken too an art form.

Lady Slippers Part 3

The best drag bar was a bar north of Boston called the Green Apple. Its patrons were a true potpourri of people, from the well-bred to the ill- mannered, a wonderful hodgepodge of characters, as if they had just stepped out of a Toulouse Lautrec painting, a poor man's Moulin Rouge. I loved it. It featured most of the famous professional female impressionists of the time. A few of the entertainers were beautiful and very natural, and I envied them. They would have had no problem existing anywhere in the world, but the entertainment was still based on illusion and titillation, and there had to be something more than that.

As enjoyable as it was, most of the humor was unfamiliar to me, and I just didn't get it, which highlighted my own ignorance, but one incident still tickles me. Many cross-dressers frequented the Green Apple, some with their wives. The problem came when people needed to go to the bathroom. Most used the men's room, They were men in dresses which was no big deal, but a few adventurous souls used the lady's room, usually without incident. I was passing by when I heard a painful grunting noise coming from the lady's room. A corpulent middle-aged lady was standing at the door cajoling its occupant, "Come on Elaine, hurry up!" The occupant answered back in a rather husky voice, "I can't, I have a prostate problem." The lady covered her eyes, shook her head and mumbled "Oh Jesus." I started laughing, and responded, "Now there's something you don't usually hear coming from the lady's room."

The Green Apple was fun. I spent time there because it was fun and I didn't feel alone. I did meet some very interesting people which taught me a great deal about respect for other people's differences, but nothing about anything else, such as social and support groups, or learn more about the non-erotic, even spiritual aspects of cross-dressing, or even changing one's sex. In time tolerance and respect for others would come in handy, but it didn't teach me anything about the spectrum of or the why's and wherefores of cross-dressing, or whatever. I didn't even know what the whatever was, so how could I do any teaching or outreach if I didn't know anything? I didn't even have the nerve or confidence to go out cross-dressed in public. A fine teacher I'd make. It was back to the Combat Zone, scouring the bookstores, with side trips to Libraries.

Whenever I made the excursion to Boston, I'd drag Sherry with me. I did not want to go into the Zone alone. Besides it was a lot more fun with her with me. In the daytime we would look for decent information. At night we explored restaurants, or the theaters, or stayed in our hotel room, which overlooked the Zone, and listened to the police sirens and fire trucks going in and out of the Zone all night. It was like being Offenbach's Orpheus in the Underworld, trying to stay safe from Pluto.

It was getting frustrating. When I came out of the Pemi-gewasset, I came out with a spiritual revelation, I came out knowing I had a special gift, and had a sense of responsibility to use that gift in a good way, to help people.   Besides Sherry, I wasn't finding any help. Everywhere we went we found Eros Goldstripe publications, Female Mimics, 51% Female, the same erotic crap we found in Peter's Palace. We had a spark of hope in the Boston Library where we found a publication called 'Transvestites' by Mangus Hirschfeld M.D., until we found it was mostly about oddities from the 19th century, and it's full title was 'Transvestites the erotic drive to cross dress'.   That dead-ended that.

Then we found a small publication called 'The Lips of Frances'. It talked about friendship and support for cross-dressers in a secure location. It did not mention or suggest sex. It was worth checking out. What I did not take into account was the level of paranoia and fear rampant in the early 1970's. We made contact, were given directions, and the rules. To me the rules were sad. For my first visit I was required not to cross-dress, which, since I had never cross-dressed in public wasn't a problem. Next, before I entered the driveway I was told to turn off my lights, which was a strange request, for seeing a car turn off its lights before entering a driveway was bound to draw attention. Next, the house had all its curtains drawn and the house was dark, it was Gothic, like approaching Wuthering Heights at night. Next, a creepy elderly lady, that looked like the sorceress Mad Madam Mimi, Merlin's nemesis, invited us in. Sherry was told to stay in the kitchen with the other wives, while I was directed to the basement. The basement was dark and dungeon-like. I half expected a funhouse Ghost to jump out at any time. I was then directed into a pantry-sized fruit cellar where six frightened cross-dressed men sat staring at me. It was like being in a scene from the movie 'One Flew Over the Cuckoo's Nest', They sat blankly, not saying or asking anything, and neither did I.

On the way home Sherry and I compared experiences. She told me being with these women was like swimming in vitriol. She had nothing to say. They were bitter, she wasn't bitter. They were angry, she wasn't angry. They weren't even remotely supportive of their partners, she was very supportive. She had nothing to say. I had nothing to say. What a strange experience. However, it did teach me several things, such as just how deeply set fear and ignorance was, how desperately wives needed an adequate support system, and finding other people like myself was not going to be easy. Maybe I really was alone. I was feeling overwhelmed with the realization of how much research and work needed to be done.

Lady Slippers Part 4

The only thing left was to make the journey to Lee Brewster's bookstore in New York. We found Lee's in the Bowery, a fetid, crusty neighborhood populated by brooding threatening characters. It seemed natural that Lee had a few security precautions. We had to ring the buzzer and be recognized before being allowed in. Once inside it felt like a secure little island in the jungle. Lee's boutique was sequins and froufrou, a spot of 'Fredrick's of Hollywood' in downtown New York. I met Lee, a soft-spoken pleasant and courteous person, as were his assistants I met, Beebe and Vicky. I remembered Vicky from her wonderful artwork on the covers of Drag magazine. I told Beebe what I was looking for and why, and was directed to the bookstore. The bookstore was far more complete than any I had seen.   Besides the usual erotica, it included biographies, books by doctors, mental health professionals and researchers, how-to books, I purchased a collection of books, including 'The Uninvited Dilemma' by Jan Morris, 'Androgyny', 'The Transsexual Phenomenon' by Doctor Harry Benjamin, 'Sexual Signatures' by Doctor John Money,   and a selection of books and magazines by Virginia Prince, including 'Understanding Cross-dressing', 'How To Be a Woman Though Male', and a few copies of 'Transvestia', one which included Virginia's biography, and many more. It was the beginning of the Merissa Sherrill Lynn Library.

I turned into a sponge, sucking up every drop of information I could. That night as Sherry and I were lying in bed, she was playing with me, and I was hungrily thumbing through every publication I had, she said, "You know this doesn't belong here. " She was telling me I was transsexual, and I had to agree, sort of. After spending a large portion of my life debating Father Walker and my parents over religion, and studying philosophy in college for seven years, studying everyone from Socrates to Heidegger, it became my habit to question everything, and make up my own mind about everything.

There was still one driving force in my life, the intense desire to be female. When I emerged from the wilderness, I came out with the knowledge that this desire was a fundamental part of my being, and there was no need to understand why. It just was. I still had no interest in cross-dressing, or Drag, or sex, but I desperately wanted to understand myself, and be able to explain it to others.

The books helped, and they didn't help. For instance, Jan Morris's story was interesting and well written, but there was nothing in it with which I could relate. Androgyny explained the nature of a maple tree, but didn't explain me. Harry Benjamin wanted to pigeonhole people, and I wasn't going to be pigeonholed. I wouldn't admit to being transsexual, but I would admit to being transsexually inclined. John Money talked about prenatal hormonal mix, as if there were some predetermined biological explanation for me being who and what I was. Bullshit. I took full responsibility for my actions, and the consequences of my actions, and would never admit to being predestined to be who and what I was. Besides, if I was predestined, it wasn't important.   It didn't matter. What did matter was that I existed, whatever the reason.

Virginia was far more perplexing. She tried to separate cross-dressing from sex, but from what I could see, was sex was what it was all out. It was a turn-on ......, period! She did emphasize full personality expression, hence the initials for her organization F.P.E. Cross-dressing was like a circus car filled with clowns. Open the doors and out pop a thousand forms of expression. It was a marvelous therapeutic oppor-tunity. Get dressed and become someone else for a while. For me the journey was spiritual, not a search for expression, and not sex. Clearly though, sex was part of it. That divided the cross-dressing/transsexual phenomena into three aspects, personal expression, the spiritual, which in some persons could produce a religious experience, and sex. Virginia's contention that cross-dressers were predominantly hetero-sexual, also made sense, from both a personal expression, and a sexual point of view. If women were what they admired, then emulation of women was natural, and vise a versa. Sexually speaking if femininity was the turn-on, then masculinity didn't enter into it. If the attempt to feel attractive to a man, the only man they were trying to turn-on was themselves.

I also applauded Virginia's efforts to separate the act of cross-dressing from being gay, and to build support and education for wives families. My depressing experience at the Lips of Frances gathering made that need manifest. My problem came when Virginia required that members of her organization be heterosexual. Her organization was a non-sexual organization based on sexual preference. That made no sense to me whatever. If a non-heterosexual or transsexually inclined person wanted to be a member, all they would have to do is lie. Since lying was what we had to do to live in society, what had we gained?

The need for a social and supportive place for people who wished to live a heterosexual lifestyle was clear, but there was nothing that required a person to fit into that particular pigeonhole in order to participate. Just about everyone had their private pigeonholes. The thought of serving all those pigeonholes separately was mind boggling. All I could think of was Pete Seeger's wonderful song 'Little Boxes' which made fun of the requirement of putting people into little boxes in order to function.

I admired Virginia, and was inspired by her efforts, but she lived and thought in a different world. I still didn't have a clue as to who or what I was, but I had enough information to put together a plausible outline and to speak at colleges and make a fool of myself. Which I did, with alacrity.

The biggest fool I made of myself was at my alma mater, the University of New Hampshire. They were sponsoring an alternative lifestyle conference, and I was asked to speak. I had been at UNH a few times before to talk to classes. I was hit with the same tired questions, "Was I gay?" "Why wasn't I cross-dressed?" I gave them the same tired answers, "I didn't know what gay meant. Since I wasn't really sexually attracted to anyone, I really didn't know how to answer that," and "As to cross-dressing in public, I was still a neophyte, and not quite ready to go prancing around in public." In the end, I received the usual courteous applause, and was about to leave, when I was approached by a reporter. She looked like a grown-up Little Orphan Annie, right down to her denim jumper, and Afro-styled red hair. She also wore wire-rimmed glasses which gave the impression of eyeballs without pupils. She really did look like Orphan Annie, or maybe Raggedy Ann, the mop doll. I assumed she was the campus newspaper, and was asking some intelligent questions with which I was comfortable.

I was hungry, and invited her to dinner at the New England Center, a beautiful nature-green hexagonal structure, designed to fit in the landscape. They had actually gone so far as to remove the pine needles from the construction site, and replaced them when construction was finished. Boardwalks were built around the trees, and each table had a panoramic view of the out-of-doors. It was beautiful, and my favorite place on campus.

We chatted, and I shared my life story, especially being afraid and being an outsider in my own family and in my community. I especially talked about my epiphany in the

Pemigewasset. I then shared some before and after pictures of myself, which she asked if she could keep. Without thinking, I said sure. We had a delightful conversation, and delightful company. I just wasn't prepared for what was about to happen.

Lady Slippers Part 5

Satisfied with the day, I went home for a few days before I went back north to go back to work. I woke up to find myself front page news in the Manchester Union Leader, the paper Robert Kennedy called the worst newspaper in America. The Union Leader, God, The Leader was still defending Joe McCarthy, and every Commie hating kook in the country.

The Leader, especially its publisher William Loeb, hated the effete intellectual snobs found at colleges. He wanted blind obedience to a nationalistic philosophy that died with McCarthy. And, I was on the front page of his newspaper. My life was over. I had just been outed by the worst paper in the country. I was far more famous than I ever wanted to be.

Not only was I on the front page, my before and after pictures were full frame over several columns of text, with the headline "Southwick (my previous name) sees both sides." How much worse could it be? I went to play bridge that night. Everyone stared at me, some congratulated me on my courage, but most just stared. My partner just reached over and stroked my arm which was now hairless. Once I was rather ape-like. To my relief, everyone was pleasant and courteous. The next day would be the real test, I had to go back to work.

It's nearly impossible to explain the anxiety. Waterville Valley, where I worked, was a conservative family oriented ski area. I was certain I was going to be fired, and had absolutely no idea what I would do after I was fired. During the trip back north, besides wondering how I allowed myself to get into this mess, there were times I was shaking so hard I wondered if I would make it.

When I arrived at the mountain, my hands were sweaty and stuck to the steering wheel. My eyes were nearly closed by salty tears, and my skin was waxy. When I approached the lodge, Werner, my boss, a fugitive from the Swiss National Ski Team, was standing by the door, a copy of the Leader in his hand. I almost turned around and went home. When I got to Werner he looked at me as if I were about to be spanked, and spoke to me in his rich Swiss accent. "I chust don't know vye you do zees things. Und, I don't care. I care about Vaterwille Walley," (I love that pronunciation) "So if dis hurts Vaterwille in any vay, you leave, OK?" I wasn't fired, thank God. "OK!"

That season was the strangest I ever experienced as a professional ski instructor. I met several members of Waterville's staff who were also cross-dressers, and a plethora of people asking to take lessons from me personally. For some reason I inherited the staff of Channel 4. Ethel Kennedy and her family were assigned to me, as were a number of celebrities who were friends of the area manager. Also a lot of husbands hired me to ski with their wives, and a lot of late 30ish wives, ladies we called 'Steamers', hired me. Besides my overload of private lessons, I had my usual ski weekers, vacationers we called 'Squeekers'. I was averaging 8-10 hours a day on a pair of skis, seven days a week for 135 consecutive days. By the end of the season my proclivities were forgotten, and I was deadly sick of skiing. At the end of the season we held a party for the instructors, where we gave out joke awards. Since I generated the most income for the Ski School, they gave me Waterville's Greatest Ass-et award. It was just a piece of paper with a picture of somebody's derriere on it, a joke, but I was, and still am, proud of it. For me the season was extremely successful.

A TRIBUTE TO ELLEN

Ellen Summers passed away in December, 1994. Simply stated, Ellen was one of the finest human beings I had ever known.

The last time I saw Ellen was on Saturday night, March 19, 1994, the night she became the eighth recipient of IFGE's Virginia Prince Lifetime Service Award. I had never seen her happier, more beautiful, or more proud than she was that night. That is how I chose to remember her.

A word about the Virginia Prince Award. I created the award to honor Virginia, and ensure the memory of the pioneers whose years of effort and leadership made our community possible, and made our positive work in education and in the public arena possible. I chose to name the award after Virginia because of the profound respect I had for her, and that virtually every good thing that existed in our community could trace its roots back to Virginia. She was the catalyst for it all.

The night Ellen received her award was a night of irony. The first irony was I was the second recipient of the award. At the time I received it, Ellen was chair of IFGE's Awards Committee, and it was her responsibility to present the award to me. I told her, "I give the awards, I don't receive them." She responded, "This time my dear, you don't have a damned thing to say about it, so shut up, receive your acknowledgement gracefully, and sit down." That night it was my turn to present the award to Ellen, so I playfully told her, "This time she didn't have a damned thing to say about it, so shut up, receive your acknowledgement gracefully, and sit down." She understood the comment.

The next irony reflected directly on Ellen, the person. The 1994 IFGE Convention was held in Oregon, at the Portland Hilton. The night of the awards was held in the Hilton Ballroom, which was filled with over 300 people resplendent in their gowns and tuxedos, all there to honor Ellen. Ellen's wife Pattie and daughter Susie were seated in the front row. The lights were dim, the music was classical, the flowers were magnificent, and our spirits soared. The walls of the ballroom were lined with members of the hotel staff who had come to join us for a single purpose, to honor Ellen Summers. When Ellen stood to speak I felt a joy in my heart and tears in my eyes, and looked around to see if anyone else felt the same. Apparently everyone felt the same, especially the hotel staff, and therein lay the irony.

Several years earlier, Ellen was thrown out of the Hilton for being cross-dressed. Two years earlier our ability to hold a convention in Portland at all was in doubt because no hotel would have us. Ellen and her friend Roni, both transgender leaders in the Northwest, went to work. Soon we not only had hotels willing to have our business, we had the best hotels in town, including the Portland Hilton, competing for our business. Ellen and Roni even went as far as conducting educational seminars for the Hilton staff. Thanks to Ellen's courage, persistence, patience, and quality of character, she went from being thrown out of the hotel, to being respected and honored by those who had rejected her. The very fact that she was able to stand, with dignity, in the spotlight of the Portland Hilton Ballroom to receive the transgender community's highest award, midst the din of applause from the Hilton staff, made manifest that no one on earth deserved the award more.

As the second recipient of the Virginia Prince Award, it was my responsibility and honor to present Ellen with her plaque, and say a few words. Since Ellen was one of the people in the transgender community, and for whom I held in the highest esteem and one of my dearest friends, saying what was in my heart with just a few words was not going to be easy. Knowing she was ill and that this could very possibly have been the last time we saw each other, made it even harder. So, I stood up, told a few personal stories about Ellen, told her I loved her, started crying, gave her a huge hug, and sat down. I hoped I would never have to do anything that difficult again.

Ellen came into my life in 1978. By that time I had already established the Tiffany Club and had made contact with hundreds of people from around the world. At first I thought she was just one more person looking for information. It became immediately clear that Ellen Summers was someone special. At no time did she dwell on what I could do for her. Instead, she wanted to know what she could do for me, and what we could do together to help other people. She was my kind of person, a kindred spirit. Perhaps most importantly in those early years Ellen brought to me her nurturing spirit, a spirit that empowered and encouraged me. There is no better way to put this, but Ellen Summers had become both my sister and my mom. I soon learned that Ellen's nurturing spirit, her ability to empower and encourage others, was the greatest gift she brought to the transgender community. She could get people to lead, to work, and to work together, and ability I hold in awe to this day.

That ability struck home with me the day we first met. That day was in June 1982, at the Crown & Anchor Motel (the C&A), in Provincetown (P-town) Massachusetts. I was coordinating the Tiffany Club's second annual Ptown outing, and Ellen was my guest of honor. A moment came midst the chaos that enabled me to sneak off with my new friend and share a quiet lunch. We went to the Steak & Lobster, an open canopied restaurant on the top deck of the C&A. We became so engrossed in our conversation we hardly noticed the storm which was rolling in off the harbor. The winds blew, hail pounded the deck and the canopy, and the restaurant staff hurried around us tying things down before the restaurant blew away. Ellen and I stoically sat there, plucking hailstones from our lobster rolls as we talked. We talked of what was being done, and of what could be done, and how we could do it. By the end of the weekend she had me doing backflips. Well, I wasn't actually doing backflips, but she had me believing that I could have if I wanted to.

ELLEN part 2

Ellen did for me what I couldn't do for myself. She had me believing in myself, and that all things were possible. From then on Ellen became far more than an advisor, a friend, and mom. She became a working partner. As the years went by I became more aware of the positive effects of Ellen's nurturing spirit. That spirit was there when she co-founded Portland's Northwest Gender Alliance (NWGA), and supported the development of Seattle's support group Emerald City. It was especially there when we ran into our little problem at the Chicago Gender Alliance's Spring Fling.

The Spring Fling was held in May 1985, at the Rodeway Inn in Rosemont, Illinois. Ellen was my roommate. The problem with the event was the event's coordinator never told the Inn's management who or what we were, and never asked for an area to be set aside for us. To make matters worse, the event coordinator never told us, the participants, that she had never told them. The Rodeway management, not knowing any better, randomly assigned rooms, which meant our participants were scattered all over the Inn. The Inn's management, also not knowing any better, rented rooms to high school hockey teams which were in town for a tournament. We found ourselves, without prior warning, surrounded by high school hockey players, their families and coaches.

We were trapped. It was like being thrown into the arena with the lions and tigers. Fear swept the Inn, but it wasn't our fear. It was the parents, coaches and hockey players who were terrified of us. Ellen, who to my knowledge had never been seen in public without a smile, went about making friends, and making it easy for people to talk to her and ask questions. Soon our room was filled with teenagers, coaches, moms and dads, chattering away like old friends, and with laughter. Ellen had taken a potentially dangerous situation and turned it into a winner. The hockey players named her after a popular movie of the time, and since then Ellen was officially known as Mister Mom.

At the second Gender Alliance's Spring Fling, I gained a greater insight into her character. 1986 was a chaotic time for me. I was in the process of turning over the management of my support group, the Tiffany Club, to its board of directors, about to launch our new organization, the International Foundation for Gender Education (IFGE), in the process of converting my magazine, the TV/TS Tapestry, into an international publication and IFGE's official publication, and making final plans for IFGE's first Coming Together Convention, which was to be held in Chicago in 1987.

We were at the Howard Johnson's Hotel in Skokie, Illinois. That year the event coordinator had the foresight to tell the hotel management who we were and what we needed.

That meant those of us who were there to work could do so without interruption, or fearing for our lives. Ellen was there, as were Yvonne Cook, a leader from Indiana, Sheila Kirk, a leader from Pittsburgh, Naomi and Eve, both leaders from Chicago, and many others. Ellen kept us together, and made our work sessions a joy.

No work could be done without coffee and donuts. We ordered a pot of coffee and a dozen donuts for Ellen, and a pot of coffee and a dozen donuts for the rest of us. I don't believe I've ever seen anyone drink more coffee, or love donuts more than Ellen. I read a tribute to Ellen written by her friend and co-leader in the northwest, Judy Osborne, in which she said, "Ellen's truest loves were family, friends, our community, and donuts." I concurred.

Ellen's dry sense of humor made her a joy to be near. She could make me laugh, and did so frequently. For instance, we were in Houston for a convention, and during a luncheon, we were sitting together at the head table. Sheila Kirk was the mistress of ceremonies. Ellen already had me laughing when Sheila began to introduce the head table. "And on my right is Dr. Virginia Prince, for whom the Virginia Prince Award is named after." Ellen, leaned toward me, and with a perfect deadpan expression said, "No shit." She said it quietly, but just loud enough for the microphone to pick it up. Everyone heard it, but no one wanted to be the first to admit they heard it, especially me. I fought off the urge to laugh, but the harder I tried, the worse the urge. Unable to hold it any longer, I lost it. When I lost it, Sheila lost it. When Sheila lost it, everyone lost it. Lunch became a shambles. Without losing a beat, or her deadpan expression, she turned to me and gave me a satisfied wink.

In 1990, Ellen, Roni, and a few other leaders from the Northwest, sponsored what they hoped would become an annual event. They called their event 90 in 90, they hoped to attract at least 90 people in 1990. They did a bit better than that. Since I had invited Ellen to be the guest of honor at one of Tiffany's outings, Ellen returned the favor and invited me to be her guest of honor, an invitation I was pleased to accept.

One of the staff members of the Ingersoll Center, a gender clinic in Seattle, met me, and she showed me around Seattle, which was a beautiful city. It was, however, exactly what they said it was, damp and misty. Wet! We took a ferry across Puget Sound and drove up the west side of the Olympic Peninsula to Port Angeles, on the peninsula's northern edge. I had heard the Olympic Peninsula was the wettest place in North America, but to my surprise, the eastern side of the peninsula was semi-arid, complete with cactus. We were in some kind of a weird rain-shadow weather pattern type of effect. That changed when we reached Port Angeles. The west side of town was wet, the east side was dry.   Weird.

The motel we were staying at had a lovely view of the Juan De Fuca Strait. I had dinner with Ellen, when she introduced me to a chunk of rubber she called gueduck. She said it was a giant clam. I still believed in snow snakes, so not knowing any better, I tried to eat it. It was good exercise for the jaw muscles, but not bad tasting. A bit like calamari. Was it calamari? Abalone? Giant clam? Goodyear steak? Deep fried Bath-mat?   I didn't know.

During lunch I was invited to stand up and say few words. Nobody told me I had to say something. Coming up with something to say when I had nothing to say was difficult, so I winged it. I thanked everybody, praised Ellen, praised the '90 in 90' event, tried to make a connection with '90 in 90' and the other events springing up all over the country, felt like a complete ass, and sat down. It was a dubious interaction with the folks in the Northwest.

One of the scheduled events was an excursion to Victoria, the capital of British Columbia on Vancouver Island, for a tour of the city and high tea at the Empress Hotel. We shared our ferry ride with a Jehovah's Witnesses youth group. No one tried to sell me anything religious, and we made it to Victoria unscathed.

When we reached Victoria, the sky was grey, and the air was a fine mist. We boarded an open sided trolley. The trolley was being drawn by two large Percheron draft horses named Chester and Benny. Victoria was beautiful, ablaze with blooming orange azaleas. For some reason the damp air seem to set the flowers on fire, making Victoria a bit more beautiful. Then Chester, who was having a bit of a digestive problem, lifted his tail and lit off a whopper. A large gas cloud floated over the left side of the trolley. There was a lot of gagging, and prolific profanity, with people diving to the right side of the trolley. Those of us on the right side of the trolley thought the whole situation was hysterically funny. Ellen, who was on the left side, ducked and dove, ending up in my lap. I warned her of exigent positions, and we waited until the gas cleared. The driver profusely apologized, Chester behaved himself, and we continued on to the Empress.

High tea was a hoot. We dove into the dainty little cucumber and watercress sandwiches, the scones and jam, the little very proper little cakes, and tea. We all played the part of proper 19th century Victorian ladies, and had a blast. A few of the Chester victims understandably waited outside. Their aroma was not Chanel #5, but Chester #1.

The last day of the event we drove up to Olympic National Park for a spectacular view of Mount Olympus, the mountains, and the deep snow pack which was still way over my head. I couldn't resist jumping on the snow pack for a little shoe skiing. I was soaked, but I loved it.

In 1991 Ellen received the Trinity Award.   The Trinity was an award I created to recognize and honor our community's heroes, people who went out into the public and made a difference, educators, writers, broke down barriers to ignorance and intolerance, saved lives, and such.   The Trinity was named after the logo I made for the Tiffany Club, of being in balance with masculinity, femininity and nature.   It was hard for me to think about Ellen without emotion, without laughter or tears.   Therefore, for me it was more gratifying to see her win the Trinity Award than the Virginia Prince Award.   Ellen was certainly a pioneer for our community, but the Trinity was for those who had performed extraordinary acts of courage and love.   To me Ellen was courage and love.   No one exemplified those qualities better.

Wednesday evening, April 10, 1991, in the Number 10 Downing Room of the Regency Hotel in Denver, In honor of her countless acts of love and courage, the transgender community made Ellen Summers the first recipient of the Trinity Award.

As Judy Osborne pointed out, Ellen was devoted to her family, and loyal to her friends.   I thank my lucky stars.   Together, Ellen and I dreamed the dreams and shared the work that made IFGE possible.   Ellen served IFGE as a cofounder, as vice-chair of the Board, on the executive committee, as chair of the nominations and awards committee, and as chief confidant and advisor.   It seemed I never did anything without first talking it over with Ellen.   Besides sharing a dream and seeing that dream to fruition, she was my friend.

Her insight and that friendship saved me, and very possibly saved IFGE.

By 1991 IFGE had become very successful. With that success came a new breed of leader, young Turks fresh from the arrogant mean spirited world of business. Idealistic dreamers such as myself became, well, pass These new leaders brought new dreams to replace the old, which meant the old had to go, which meant I had to go. I was well aware of my lack of business skills, and lack of interest in business. To me the bottom line was how much good did we do. To the young Turks the bottom line was profit. These bottom lines were fundamentally antithetical. However, I was also well aware that if I were forced out, then my dreams would be forced out, and the heart would have been torn out of IFGE. In effect, IFGE would have died, and I could not allow that to happen. A rift developed within IFGE, a rift that could easily have destroyed everything we had worked so hard for.

At the January 1993 IFGE Board of Directors meeting, the then chair of the Board took ma aside, and aggressively told me, "If you don't get out of the way there will be blood on the convention floor." They were not going to budge, I was not going to budge, and the stage was set for a showdown at the Philadelphia '93 convention in March. I was seriously considering scrapping it all, and starting again from scratch. Our focus and IFGE's reason for being was being lost, buried in bullshit.

We arrived in Philadelphia during the 'storm of the century'. Blizzards had hit the east coast from Georgia to the Maritimes. Philadelphia was buried under an 18" blanket of wet snow, as heavy as concrete. It was a wonder anybody made it at all. Everyone was there. There had already been considerable damage done, friendships destroyed, and we were steeled for battle.

There was a gloom hanging over the convention, that was ominous and ugly. In stepped Ellen. I had always loved and trusted Ellen, but I truthfully did not know her real power until that convention. She took us all aside, like so many naughty children, sat us down, and said, "NO!!!!" No meant no, and that was that. Mother Superior had spoken. "Now let's work it out." Work it out meant work it out. That was the first time any of us were able to get over our hubris, and look for ways we could work together.

Unfortunately they still wanted me to take their orders, and I wanted them to understand IFGE's purpose, and that chain-of-command and quest for profit were not the way. We could see that we needed someone who could coordinate IFGE's business affairs. We needed an executive director. That wasn't me. We also needed someone who had a clear understanding of the "big picture," and could keep us going in the right direction. we needed a founding director. That was me. With that clearly understood and agreed upon, we were finally able to make a little headway to finding compromise, and start healing wounds. So, in one wonderful act of authority and diplomacy, Ellen saved me, saved IFGE, became IFGE's Mother Superior, and its Supreme Judge Advocate, the final authority.

ELLEN part 4

During the Philadelphia convention Ellen was in constant pain. I knew it, as did a few others, but she never let it show. She never stopped working, she never stopped trying to help, and she never let anyone else take her place. I scolded her, trying to get her rest, but clearly she had more power over me, than I did over her.

On Saturday she suffered through a long Board meeting, then through a long Awards Banquet. She should have been resting, but insisted on being there to support the seventh recipient of the Virginia Prince Award, her friend, Carol Beecroft. The next day she came to the farewell brunch, bent over with pain. She came to receive the IFGE Football,

There-by accepting responsibility to coordinate the host committee for the 1994 convention. There was some question as to whether or not she would even love to see another convention, yet there she was, accepting the responsibility to coordinate the host committee.

The next year, thanks to Ellen, the Portland '94 convention was a fantastic success, and she herself became the recipient of the Virginia Prince Lifetime Service Award. No one was more deserving.

To me success is when on your deathbed you can say, with complete honesty, that the world is a better place because you lived. The world is a far better place because Ellen Summers lived.

THE CANDLES

The Candles part 1

This installment was intended to be a memorial for friends who had died. In respect for their memory, and in respect for those who may yet remember them, I have changed their  names.   However, the people mentioned here were very real. The lone exception was Lou Sullivan, who had a special effect on my life. I wanted to remember them in a good way, and to think of them as 'spirit teachers', to ensure their memories would not be forgotten, and their lives would not have been wasted.

As it was with the first New Women's Conference, the second New Woman's Conference was also held at the Essex Conference Center in Essex, Massachusetts. Also, as with the first conference, the objective was a celebration for those of us who had completed our surgeries, and survived to reach our goals as new women.

The conference started well enough, with Rachel, a celebrity in our small community, an original participant in the NYC Stonewall Riots which began the liberation movement for the gay and transgendered communities, and a regular tour guide to the ancient Hellenic cultures of the Aegean, conducting a spiritual seminar. Her theme was relating to the natural world, a theme I could personally relate to very well. Unfortunately, during the session Rena fell asleep. In her sleep she farted. It wasn't a blast, rather, a sweet little peep, so subtle only those of us close to her could hear it. I could feel myself start to laugh, but I tried to repress it, in respect for Rachel. The harder I tried to repress my impulse to laugh, the harder it got. Finally I had to get up and leave, disrupting Rachel's session. I made it to the stairs and exploded into a maniacal fit of laughter. It was very, very, embarrassing which made it that much funnier. Evelyn was downstairs playing her hammer dulcimer, an instrument I loved. Evelyn was a professional street musician, having regularly played at Renaissance Fairs and in tourist towns such as Provincetown and Bolder, across the country. I wanted to enjoy her music, but I couldn't stop laughing, so I bought all her tapes. Rena came downstairs, having realized what she had done and joined me in my laughing convulsion. We couldn't stop. Rachel came downstairs, and in a reference to the theme of her session, said, "Methane is natural too." That got us all laughing, even Evelyn who had no idea what was happening.

At dinner one of the women wanted to enrich our conference experience and suggested we had a candlelight memorial ceremony to remember those of us who had not survived to reach their goals. She had brought several boxes of hurricane candles for the occasion. After dinner, we retreated back upstairs to the conference room.

The night was perfect for a memorial ceremony ... cool and dark, with a damp salty breeze drifting in from the ocean. Twenty four of us entered the large empty room and formed a circle, then sat cross-legged on the floor with our candles. The person two places from me lit her candle, then counter-clockwise, one at a time each of us lit our candles from hers. The room became a little brighter but still very somber.

She began the ceremony by saying, "I would like to begin by remembering two of my sisters from my support group.

My friend Sharon was desperate to have surgery. The day after she learned that was not possible, she was found hanging in her garage. My best friend Dale was murdered. She was the victim of a hate crime. Some guy came up and took her for a prostitute, and beat her to death." She spoke slowly pausing occasionally to wipe tears from her eyes, telling us who they were, how she remembered them, and how she felt. Then, almost as an afterthought, she remembered three more of her friends who died, one from a drug overdose and two from AIDS. She then blew her candle out. The next person to speak remembered eight of her friends, most of whom died of AIDS, two by suicide, and her best friend by murder. Somebody used a broomstick and impaled her.

The next person had been an active member of the Fire Island community, and had come to the conference after attending her 137th funeral. It was clear that all of us had too much pain and sadness in our lives, and knew too much death. There were twenty four of us. It would have taken forever to tell our stories, so we limited ourselves to four of our favorite remembrances apiece. Then, moving counter-clockwise around the room, each of us told our stories in turn.

Each story was powerful, heartfelt, and beautiful in its way. People were talking about people they loved, friends who met misfortune, people they tried to help, or those who were beyond help. Every story was moving, and every story was different. Like everyone else, with each story I felt a lump in my throat and tears in my eyes. I also wondered who I would remember, and what I would say. I wanted to talk about Sherry, because I loved her and she loved me, in spite of who and what I was, and because I was who I was. She was also a friend of the community, but not a member of the community. I thought it more relevant to keep my comments to members of our community we have lost.

When it came my turn to speak, I began, "For many years now, I've devoted my life to helping our people. During that time I've known a lot of people who have died, far too many to remember here tonight. I would like to remember four people whose deaths had a profound effect on my life, and on my work."

"The first person I would like to remember was a Boston University college student. From the time I emerged from my own closet until I founded the Tiffany Club and IFGE, I worked on my own issues while using my own angst as a motivation to help others like myself. Early on I began receiving phone calls from a young college student. We talked, or more accurately she talked about her transsexualism, and about the pressures of school, and of being rejected by her family. She talked about her depression, and how frustrated she was trying to get some relief from her therapist. In a frighteningly sad voice she told me she had just returned from her therapist. He had told her he couldn't do anything for her, and their professional relationship was over. When she told me that, I had an alarming feeling that her therapist had just condemned her, and I had just become the only support she had in the world. I became desperate to help her, told her I would come to Boston for her, anything, but all she said was 'Goodbye.'"

"It was the most unnerving 'goodbye' I ever heard. I didn't know what to do, so I called Samaritans a suicide hotline, asking for help. They didn't know what to do either. That night was terrible, praying she would call, but knowing she wouldn't. A few days later the News carried a notice of a college student, my student, who had committed suicide. The issue wasn't that a student had died, but that the student was male and wearing a dress. That was the news, not that a troubled young man was dead but that he was wearing a dress.   Big deal, and for the news people it was a big deal.

The lessons this student taught me were first, society had to grow up, learn some tolerance and understanding, and change it's attitude, and that was going to happen only if our people, me, went out and helped teach them.   Next, she taught me that we couldn't save everyone.   Therefore, we, I, must have the fortitude to focus on those we could help, and let go of those we could not.   For that to happen, we, I, had to build a community, a support network that would support each of us as supported each other.   Next, she taught me helping professionals weren't always uncaring monsters, but like most of us in the beginning were ignorant.   We needed to build a network of skilled professionals who could actually help.   In order to do that, we, I, needed to learn and be able to teach, to help those mental health professionals to do a better job.   It was not enough to focus on just helping our people.   It was up to us, me, to build a better educational and support network.   If my student had had decent therapy, and adequate knowledge and support, perhaps she would not have died.   She helped put me on my life's path, and as a result the Tiffany Club, the Wayland House, the Tapestry, IFGE, the Coming-Together convention, and the rest of it came into being."

"The next person I would like to remember is Laura.   Laura was an active member of the Tiffany Club, a good friend, and a good friend of my niece, whom I treasured.   By the time Laura came along, I had met thousands of people, and run more conventions and outings, and coordinated more parties than I cared to remember.   Laura was smart and funny, and she was my friend.   She also was a spitfire, wired and full of energy.   She considered herself 'transsexual' and had an 'I want what I want, and I want it now' attitude, and that was that.   She was like a squirrel grabbing for all the acorns she could in the shortest period of time. Unfortunately there was no gender clinic to help her through transition, and more importantly, no work had been done to improve the workplace and no good information on how to deal with work. She just wasn't able to deal with living two lives, one in the world and one at work. She was on her own. At the time she had an excellent and well-paying job as a programmer for a top computer company. She thought it proper to inform her employers of her intentions. She had no guidelines, so she went about telling them in her usual style, with both guns blazing."

"For me personally, I had been outed by a newspaper, and was fortunate to have had a tolerant boss. Laura was not so fortunate. Her employers fired her on the spot. Laura disappeared. No one knew what had happened to her, but we all prayed she would be all right, and would come back to us. Several months later the news stations all carried the story of a red Pinto being pulled from the Charles River Basin. In the trunk of the car they found the body of a man wearing women's clothes. It was Laura. She had been viciously and brutally stabbed and beaten to death. From a valuable and well paid employee to a murder victim in a few short months."

"I cried for days. What an incredible heart-breaking waste. Because of ignorance and intolerance in the workplace, a business lost a valuable employee. Because of my inability to help, and provide an adequate support system, I lost a sister and a friend. Through no fault of her own, my niece lost a friend. Because of her impatience and lack of knowledge, Laura lost her life in a very ugly way."

"She taught me any things. She taught me respect for the power of desperation, and how easy it was for desperate peowhich meant we were all in danger. She taught me the importance of building bridges to the workplace, that civilians and family need support as well. We, I, had to do a better job reaching out to help the family, the employer and society. Laura taught me how truly important that work was."

The Candles Part 3

"The next person I would like to remember is Sheila. She was a plain old All-American cross-dresser, and absolutely l ple to do desperate things. She reinforced the importance of providing adequate knowledge and support. If Laura, a skilled professional person, can so easily place herself in terminally dangerous situations, then anyone can, oved to cross-dress. She respected me for what I was, and I respected her for what she was, and we were friends. More importantly, she was close friends with my sister, who was also a seamstress. When I met her, she was a successful advertising executive with her own business, and had a wife and children. Unfortunately, she had a terrible time dealing with her compulsion to cross-dress. She was extremely unhappy and constantly afraid she was going to be caught cross-dressed and lose everything. As a coping device, she turned to alcohol and cocaine. For some reason I have never been able to understand, she thought being an alcoholic drug abuser as more acceptable than being a cross-dresser. Of course it wasn't, and the alcohol and drugs cost her her family, and her friends. Then one day, in the late Fall, I learned Sheila had been found dead, cross-dressed, face-down on her kitchen floor, her face covered with cocaine."

"I hate drugs, and the parasites who sell it. Sheila had long ago lost my friendship and my respect because of her drug abuse. So, when I learned drugs had killed her, I was not surprised. Later I became very sad thinking of all the Sheila's out there trying to deal with their compulsion to cross-dress, family and job stress, alcoholism and drug abuse.

For Sheila, cocaine was not the cause of her death. It was the weapon."

"Sheila enjoyed cross-dressing. So what? No big deal, yet I'm constantly shocked at how big a deal people make of it. People would become workaholics, alcoholics, drug addicts and worse in order to deal with the desire to cross-dress. People, good people, were destroying themselves, and killing themselves because of it. What were we, I, doing about it? Sheila taught me that in most cases, Alcohol and substance abuse was not the problem. It was the symptom." "Finally I would like to remember Lou. Lou was a female-to-male transsexual. I never met him, never met any female-to-males before, although I occasionally met one or two at conventions, and I remember reading about Lou in the old Gateway Gender Alliance newsletters, but that was the extent of my contact. Then I learned Lou had AIDS. Then came the book 'Information For the Female-to-Male' by Louis Sullivan, and then another book 'From Female To Male, The Life Of Jack Bee Garland' by Louis Sullivan. I began to take notice. Who was this guy? I began reading articles and digging a bit into his history. What I found was a leader, a researcher, and a writer. I found an extraordinary human being who had devoted his life to making other people's lives better. I found a kindred spirit."

"When Lou died I felt sad and proud at the same time. Here was a man who knew he was going to die, yet devoted his remaining years to making this a better more enlightened world. When he died, I knew he died with the knowledge that the world was in fact a better place because he had existed. I prayed that when my time came I could say the same."

"Lou left us with one of my favorite quotes, 'I may never become a gay male, but at least I'm going to die as one.'

Lou had achieved fulfillment. Lou taught me a great lesson about giving, and about the power of human dignity. He taught me of the peace that can be found in being in balance with one's own identity. Perhaps most of all, Lou taught me to never ever forget the beauty, the talent and potential, and the humanity of our brothers.

Mount Washington, N.H.
September 15, 2018

Picture of Marci and Sharon

Merissa is at peace in a place she loved overlooking the snow fields, forest, and the mountains of New Hampshire.

Her friends said a Native American Prayer and the sun shined.

Obituary for Merissa Sherrill Lynn
1942 - 2017

Merissa was born in Exeter and lived in North Hampton, New Hampshire. She graduated from the University of New Hampshire in 1971 with a BA in Philosophy. Entered the United States Army in 1961 and served with an Army Ranger Battalion in Germany from 1961-1963 and was honorably discharged in 1964.

Ms. Lynn established a support group and meeting home for gender variant individuals in Waltham Mass at a time when gender variance was little understood, and not studied as a visible social norm. She assisted many individuals who were searching for a safe and viable place to express their choice of gender preference. Her home became one of the first national clubs or associations for cross-dressers, transgender both for male and female sexual-reassignment individuals. She established the Tiffany Club of New England as a safe zone for those looking for and needing understanding in their gender search.

From this home she published what was to become an international magazine specializing in information and contacts between social, medical, and businesses communities dealing with the transgender movement. With many groups around the world reaching out for contact she founded the International Foundation for Gender Education (IFGE) which acted as a communications network for what was to become a world-wide community. Through this organization she made contact with various other organizations and individuals who were able to make many social and legal changes in the ways people are viewed. These efforts, in combination with the Gay and Lesbian community now commonly known as LBGT, opened the door to the many social changes we see today.

Ms. Lynn's contribution to the understanding of gender variance greatly increased the knowledge and understanding available at colleges and universities worldwide. She was asked to speak at Harvard Medical School and many conferences in the US and abroad. As the director of IFGE she traveled widely to promote understanding and education about gender viability and inclusion in everyday life. She was honored by many organizations for her knowledge, writings, publications and community organization work. She gave of her time and energies to promote gender acceptance, much of what we see today commonly throughout this country.

Suffering a massive stroke in 1998, Ms. Lynn was unable to devote time and energy into the complexities of the business and moved to Warwick, RI where she has resided for the past 20 years and finally passed away at Hope Hospice on Friday Dec. 1, 2017. Her legacy is in the help she gave to many who were looking for answers to deeply personal questions. She gave hope and love to all throughout her life. She will be deeply missed by many.

Acknowledgements and Thanks:

Mariette Pathy Allen - Photographer
Dallas Denny   – Editorial Assistance
Niela Miller   - Editorial Assistance
Judy Osborne –   Editorial Assistance
Marci McNamara – Helping Friends
Sharon Barber   – Helping Friends
Karin Wells   - Helping Friend

To all of the individuals who received Merissa's original emails know that you were very special to her. Thank You.

To all who ever met, knew of, and loved Merissa Sherrill Lynn while supporting her work and dreams. Please keep her dreams going so more can have the freedom she worked so hard to obtain a much better life for all.

To all gender challenged individuals who have learned to enjoy their dual nature please keep being open and assisting others no matter what their challenges are as they also hurt the way you have hurt but lived to see better days.

A brighter day for all is important.